Microsoft® PowerPoint®
2002
fast&easy®

Check the Web for Updates:

To check for updates or corrections relevant to this book and/or CD-ROM visit our updates page on the Web at **http://www.prima-tech.com/support.**

Send Us Your Comments:

To comment on this book or any other PRIMA TECH title, visit our reader response page on the Web at **http://www.prima-tech.com/comments**.

How to Order:

For information on quantity discounts, contact the publisher: Prima Publishing, P.O. Box 1260BK, Rocklin, CA 95677-1260; (916) 787-7000. On your letterhead, include information concerning the intended use of the books and the number of books you want to purchase.

Donna Weir

Microsoft® PowerPoint® 2002

2002

fast&easy®

Coletta Witherspoon

PRIMA TECH

A Division of Prima Publishing

A Division of Prima Publishing

Prima Publishing and colophon and Fast & Easy are registered trademarks of Prima Communications, Inc. PRIMA TECH is a registered trademark of Prima Communications, Inc., Roseville, California 95661.

Publisher: Stacy L. Hiquet

Associate Marketing Manager: Heather Buzzingham

Managing Editor: Sandy Doell

Acquisitions Editor: Debby Abshier

Technical Reviewer: Joyce Nielsen

Book Production and Editorial: Argosy

Cover Design: Prima Design Team

Microsoft, Windows, and PowerPoint are either registered trademarks or trademarks of Microsoft Corporation in the United States and/or other countries.

Important: Prima Publishing cannot provide software support. Please contact the appropriate software manufacturer's technical support line or Web site for assistance.

Prima Publishing and the author have attempted throughout this book to distinguish proprietary trademarks from descriptive terms by following the capitalization style used by the manufacturer.

Information contained in this book has been obtained by Prima Publishing from sources believed to be reliable. However, because of the possibility of human or mechanical error by our sources, Prima Publishing, or others, the Publisher does not guarantee the accuracy, adequacy, or completeness of any information and is not responsible for any errors or omissions or the results obtained from use of such information. Readers should be particularly aware of the fact that the Internet is an ever-changing entity. Some facts may have changed since this book went to press.

ISBN: 0-7615-3396-6

Library of Congress Catalog Card Number: 2001086691

Printed in the United States of America

01 02 03 04 05 DD 10 9 8 7 6 5 4 3 2 1

To Craig,
Because a husband is forever.

Contents at a Glance

PART IV
CREATING SPECIAL EFFECTS 183

PART V
GETTING READY FOR THE SHOW 215

PART VI
APPENDIXES 313

Contents

Acknowledgments

To everyone at Prima Publishing: Thank you for all your hard work on the many, many books that we've done together. Special thanks go to Debbie Abshier, Caroline Roop, Eve Minkoff, Heather Moehn and Joyce Nielsen for their contributions to this book.

About the Author

Coletta Witherspoon is the author or co-author of over 20 books that range in user level from beginner to advanced, including *Quicken 2001 Fast & Easy*, *Microsoft PowerPoint 2000 Fast & Easy*, and *Microsoft FrontPage 2000 Fast & Easy*. Prior to becoming a publishing author, Coletta developed training materials for both small businesses and international corporations.

Introduction

This *Fast & Easy* guide from Prima Tech will help you master Microsoft PowerPoint and help you create and deliver informative and effective presentations. PowerPoint is a presentation design program that offers an easy way to design a slide show to fit any need. PowerPoint has been popular with users for many years, and with each new version of the program, new features have been added to make PowerPoint more user friendly and Web compatible.

PowerPoint can be easily used by anyone, even if you are not an artist or professional presenter. With PowerPoint, you can create multimedia rich presentations complete with graphics, sounds, animations, voiceovers, and slide transitions. PowerPoint presentations can be delivered on a computer, through a projector, in a kiosk, or as part of a Web site.

Who Should Read this Book?

This book is directed toward the novice computer user in need of a hands-on approach. The generous use of illustrations makes this an ideal tool for those who have never used a presentation design program before. This book is also for those who are familiar with previous versions of PowerPoint and want to rapidly apply their skills to this newest version of PowerPoint.

This book is organized so you can quickly look up tasks to help you complete a job or learn a new trick. You may need to read an entire chapter to master a subject, or you may only need to read a certain section of a chapter to get your creative juices flowing.

Becoming a Presentation Wizard

You'll notice that this book keeps explanations to a minimum to help you learn faster and get up to speed with PowerPoint quickly. Other features of this book provide more information on how to work with PowerPoint.

- Tips offer helpful hints about PowerPoint that make your job a little easier and help you create presentations efficiently.

- Notes offer additional information about PowerPoint to enhance your learning experience with the software.

- The appendix lists shortcut keys that help you make the transition from the mouse to the keyboard. You'll also find that the use of shortcut keys can increase your productivity and help you complete a presentation in less time.

Have fun with PowerPoint and make your next presentation a smashing success!

PART I

Getting Acquainted with PowerPoint

1

Understanding the Basics

Every project needs a starting point and if you are using PowerPoint for the first time, you'll want to start with a quick exploration of the program. Start up the application, look around the program window, and open a few menus. If you are upgrading from a previous version of PowerPoint, a quick look around will reveal some new features that you may find useful. In this chapter, you'll learn how to:

- Open and close PowerPoint
- Organize your work area
- Use toolbars efficiently
- Execute program commands

Starting and Stopping PowerPoint

The Microsoft Windows operating system provides a convenient way to start any program that is installed on your computer. Follow these steps for a quick and easy way to display the PowerPoint program on your screen.

1. **Click** on the **Start button** on the Windows Taskbar. The Start menu will appear.

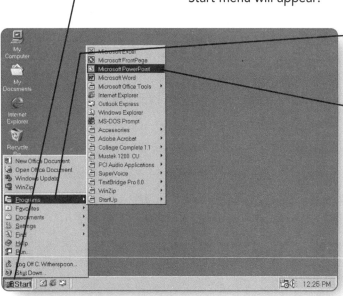

2. **Move** the **mouse pointer** to Programs. The Programs menu will appear.

3. **Click** on **Microsoft PowerPoint**. PowerPoint will open and will display a new, blank presentation.

You can start working on a new PowerPoint presentation from this blank presentation file.

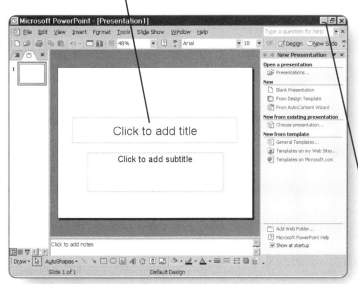

NOTE

In Chapter 3, "Learning About Presentations," you'll find out how to get a head start on your presentation with the AutoContent Wizard and the design templates.

4. Click on the **Minimize button**. PowerPoint will become an icon on the Taskbar. When you want to work with the program, click on the Taskbar icon.

Putting PowerPoint on the Desktop

If you use PowerPoint often, you can save a few mouse clicks by putting a shortcut to PowerPoint on the desktop.

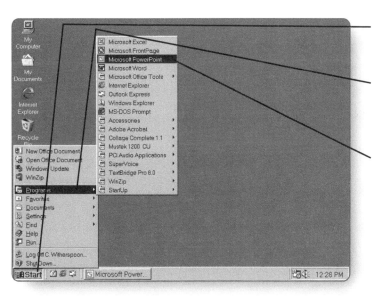

1. Click on the **Start button**. The Start menu will appear.

2. Move the **mouse pointer** to Programs. The Programs menu will appear.

3. Right-click on **Microsoft PowerPoint**. A context menu will appear.

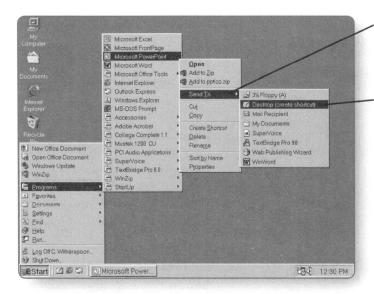

4. **Move** the **mouse pointer** to Send To. Another context menu will appear.

5. **Click** on **Desktop (create shortcut).** A confirmation dialog box will appear.

TIP

You can use these steps to create a desktop shortcut for any program that is installed on the computer.

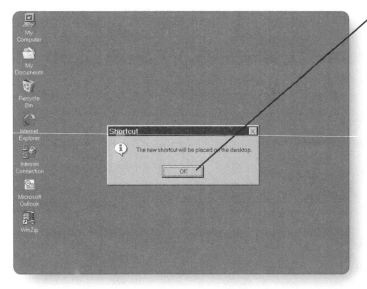

6. **Click** on **OK.** A desktop shortcut will appear on the screen.

7. **Click (or double-click depending on how you have set up the desktop)** on the **Microsoft PowerPoint shortcut**. The PowerPoint program will open.

Opening PowerPoint from Microsoft Office

You've just seen two ways to start PowerPoint. These are efficient methods if you are only working with PowerPoint. But, what do you do if you work with several programs in the Microsoft Office suite? Here's how to use the Office Shortcut Bar to start PowerPoint.

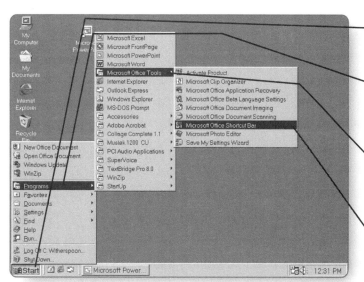

1. **Click** on **Start**. The Start menu will appear.

2. **Move** the **mouse pointer** to Programs. The Programs menu will appear.

3. **Move** the **mouse pointer** to Microsoft Office Tools. The Office Tools menu will appear.

4. **Click** on **Microsoft Office Shortcut Bar**. A confirmation dialog box will appear.

NOTE

Depending on how your copy of Microsoft Office was installed, you may be prompted to insert the Office CD so that the Office Shortcut Bar can be installed.

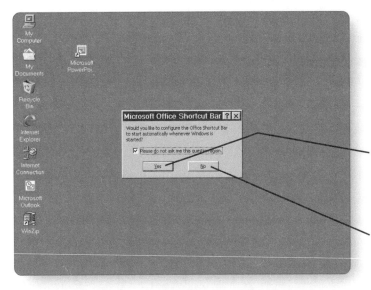

5. **Select** an **option** to decide if you want the Office Shortcut Bar to appear each time you start your computer. The Office Shortcut Bar will appear along the side of the screen.

- **Click** on **Yes**. The Office Shortcut Bar will display automatically each time you turn on your computer.

- **Click** on **No**. You will have to start the Office Shortcut Bar (using Steps 1 through 4) each time that you want to use it.

6. **Click and drag** the **Office Shortcut Bar title bar**. The Office Shortcut Bar will be moved to a different location on the screen.

NOTE

The Office Shortcut Bar will float on the screen. You can place the Office Shortcut Bar along any edge of the screen, or you can turn it into a box and place it in the middle of the screen.

7. **Click** on the **Microsoft PowerPoint icon** on the Office Shortcut Bar. PowerPoint will appear on the screen.

Closing the Program

When you are finished with PowerPoint, you'll want to save your work and close the program. These steps show you how easy it is to close PowerPoint.

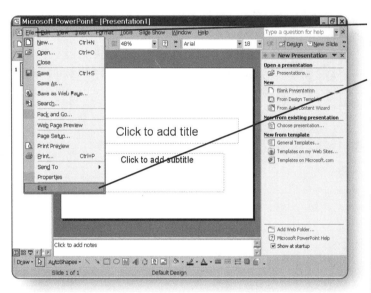

1. **Click** on **File**. The File menu will appear.

2. **Click** on **Exit**. PowerPoint will close and you can leave your computer to take a short break.

NOTE

If you have an open presentation to which you've made changes and not saved, PowerPoint will prompt you to save the file.

TIP

If you don't see the Exit command on the File menu, click the down arrow at the bottom of the menu. This will display all of the available menu commands.

Looking at Your Viewing Options

The first time you open PowerPoint, you'll see an assortment of menus, toolbars, and window panes. All of these elements combined help you create well-organized and great looking presentations. Before you begin, take a look at the PowerPoint work area where you'll create the actual design for a presentation. The PowerPoint work area can be viewed in a number of different ways. Here's what you'll find in the Normal view, which is where you'll do most of your work.

1. **Hold** the **mouse pointer** over a View button. A tooltip will appear that describes the different ways in which you can view a presentation.

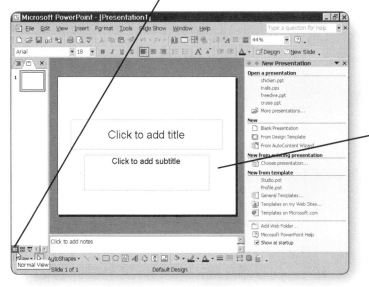

- The Normal view, which appears by default, is the most frequently used presentation view. To display this view, click on the Normal View button.

- The Slide pane is the area where you will build the individual slides. Each slide is a separate page within the presentation. Each slide can contain text, graphics, a unique background, and headers and footers.

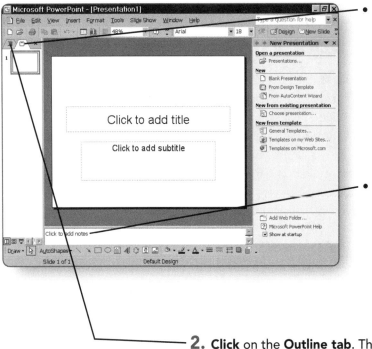

- The slide thumbnails, which can be accessed by clicking on the Slides tab, display miniature versions of each slide in a presentation. The Slides tab, like the Outline tab, can be used to organize the structure of a presentation.

- Below the Slide pane is the Notes pane. You can use this pane to keep notes that you can use during a presentation. These notes can be reminders for yourself, or an addition to any slides that are printed and used as handouts.

2. Click on the **Outline tab**. The presentation outline will appear.

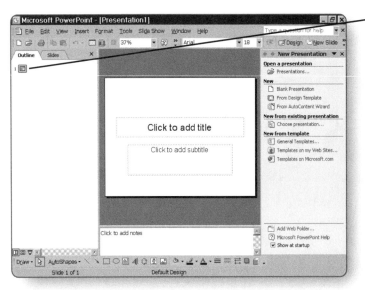

The Outline tab is used to create and edit the basic structure of a presentation. The first step in designing an effective presentation is to develop a strong outline.

> **NOTE**
>
> You'll learn how to create an outline in Chapter 4, "Organizing the Presentation Outline," and how to rearrange the slides in Chapter 5, "Shaping Up Presentation Slides."

Working with the Task Pane

A new feature that you'll find in all of the Microsoft Office programs is the Task Pane. The Task Pane is actually a number of panes that group tasks, much like the menus or toolbars. The New Presentation task pane that displays when PowerPoint first opens can be used to get a quick start on a presentation. The New Presentation task pane lists the wizards and templates that are at your command. There are a few more panes that you'll find useful and you'll learn how to use these in later chapters. For now, here's how to switch between task panes and how to hide the Task Pane.

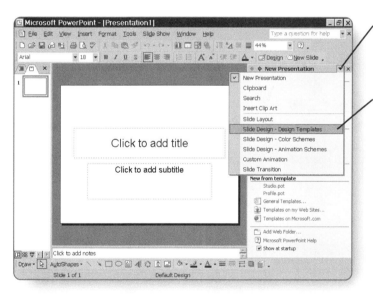

1. **Click** on the **Task Pane down arrow**. A list of available task panes will appear.

2. **Click** on a **task pane**. A new group of tasks will appear in the Task Pane.

3. Click on the **back arrow**. The previously displayed task pane (which should be New Presentation) will appear.

4. Click the **forward arrow**. Keep using the forward arrow and back arrow to display previously viewed task panes.

5. Click the **Close button**. The Task Pane will disappear. You'll notice that the work area increases in size. This gives you more room in which to design individual slides.

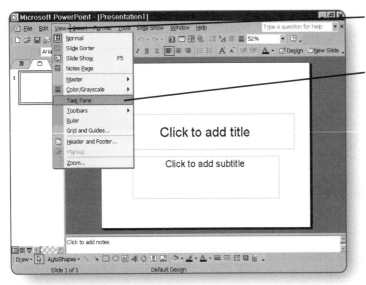

6. Click on **View**. The View menu will appear.

7. Click on **Task Pane**. The Task Pane will reappear in the PowerPoint window.

Getting a Handle on Toolbars

PowerPoint displays a number of toolbars along the top of the window. Toolbars execute commonly used commands quickly. With the click of a button, you can create a new file, save a work-in-progress presentation file, and format text. Take a few moments to learn how to use toolbar buttons to your advantage. PowerPoint displays three toolbars when the program first opens.

- The Standard toolbar contains shortcuts to frequently used file commands. From this toolbar you can save a file, print a presentation, perform a spell check, copy text, and insert tables and charts.

- The Formatting toolbar contains buttons that format text. Use this toolbar when you want to apply a different font style and size to text, change the alignment of paragraphs, or create bulleted or numbered lists.

- The Drawing toolbar makes it easy to draw shapes, add artistic effects to text, and insert pictures to a presentation.

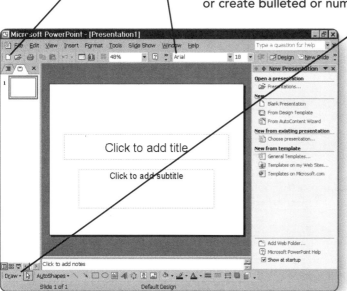

TIP

PowerPoint contains many more toolbars that help you work efficiently. To find these toolbars, open the View menu and move the mouse pointer to Toolbars.

Displaying ToolTips

Now that you've seen the toolbars that automatically appear in PowerPoint, it's time to test them out. Here's how to find out which command each Toolbar button executes.

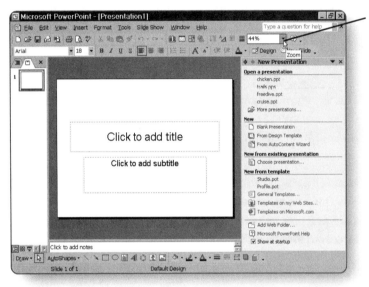

1. Hold the **mouse pointer** over a Toolbar button. A ScreenTip will appear that describes the command the button executes.

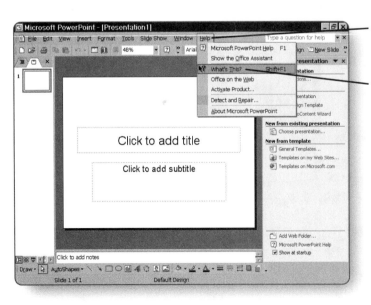

2. Click on **Help**. The Help menu will appear.

3. Click on **What's This?** The mouse pointer will change to an arrow with a question mark attached.

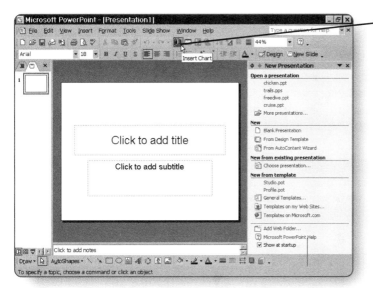

4. Click on a **Toolbar button**. A ScreenTip will appear that provides a more detailed description.

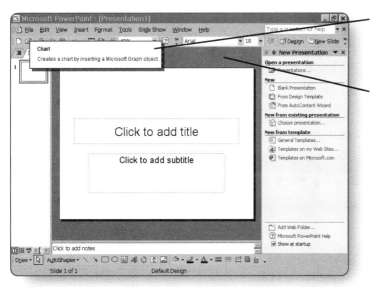

ScreenTips are a quick way to learn about the many Toolbar buttons.

5. Click on a **blank area** of the screen and outside the ScreenTip area. The ScreenTip will disappear.

Moving Toolbars

You may find that the location of toolbars is not convenient for the way in which you work. Toolbars can be moved to any location on the screen that is convenient for you. A toolbar may be docked (attached to other toolbars), or it may float all by itself on the screen.

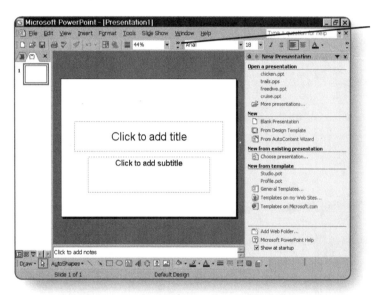

1. Click and hold the **toolbar handle**. The mouse pointer will change to a four-pointed arrow.

2. Move the **mouse pointer** to another location on the PowerPoint window. The toolbar will move with the mouse.

- A toolbar can be aligned with the menu bar or another toolbar.

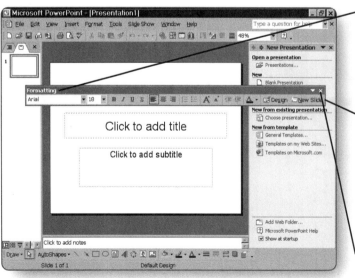

- A toolbar can be detached from the other toolbars so that it floats in the window.

TIP

Click and drag the side of a floating toolbar to reduce the width of the toolbar. The buttons will be arranged in rows.

---

3. Click on the **Close button**. The toolbar will disappear.

Introducing the Text Input Toolbar

If the Language and Speech tools are installed on your computer, you'll find some new and exciting ways to work with your computer.

NOTE

To display the Formatting toolbar (or any other toolbar), click on the View menu, move the mouse pointer to Toolbars, and click on Formatting.

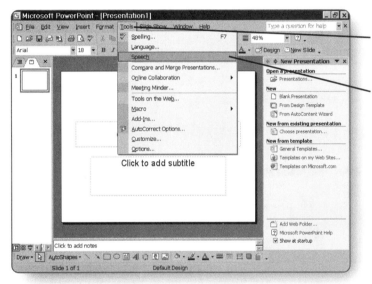

1. **Click** on **Tools**. The Tools menu will appear.

2. **Click** on **Speech**. The Text Input Settings toolbar will appear.

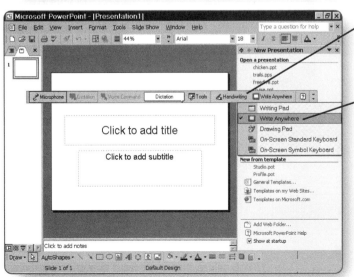

3. **Click** on **Handwriting**. The handwriting command list will appear.

4. **Click** on a **writing tool**. The tool button will appear on the toolbar.

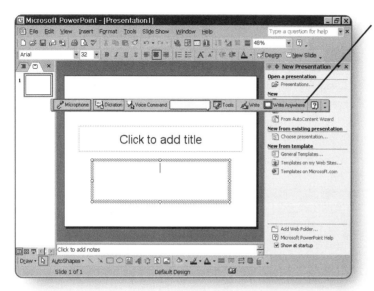

5. **Click** on the **tool**. A toolbar for the selected tool will appear on the screen.

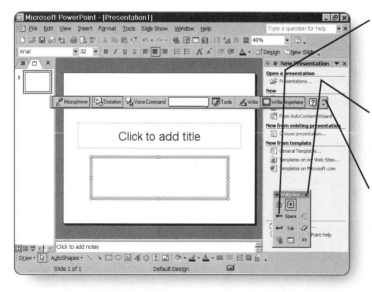

6. **Experiment** with the **tool**. If you're addicted to the mouse, you'll get a kick out of producing words with a few clicks.

7. **Click** the **Close button** when you are finished. The keyboard toolbar will disappear.

8. **Click** the **Minimize button** on the Text Input Settings toolbar. The toolbar will become an icon in the system tray (located at the right end of the taskbar).

Using Menus and Dialog Boxes

You'll find a new look in the menu system. Here's a quick look at how these new menus work and a tip about a cool dialog box trick.

1. Click on **File**. When the menu first appears, only the most frequently used commands appear in the menu list. If you wait a few seconds, the menu list will expand and show all of the commands for the File menu.

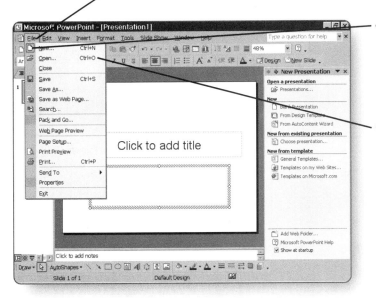

- Along the left side of the menu, you'll see a number of icons. These are the icons used on the various toolbars to indicate a command.

- Along the right is the associated shortcut key for the command. These shortcut keys are helpful if you have a difficult time using the mouse, either from a repetitive strain injury or because you are working on a laptop.

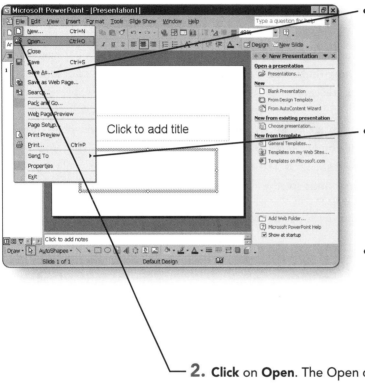

- When an ellipsis (. . .) follows a menu command, a dialog box will open when the command is executed. You'll learn more about dialog boxes in a little bit.

- A right pointing arrow on the right side of the menu lets you know that a second menu will appear when you place the mouse pointer over the menu command.

- Any time a command is grayed out, it is not available for use. There may be several reasons for this: text is not selected, a file is not open, or a feature is disabled.

2. **Click** on **Open**. The Open dialog box will open.

3. **Click and drag** the **resize handle**. The dialog box will become larger. This feature is available only in a few dialog boxes.

4. **Click Cancel**. The dialog box will close and no changes will be made.

2

Asking for Help

As you work on a presentation, you may find that every now and then you need a quick reminder on how to perform a task or some help learning an unfamiliar program feature. You have several choices. You can refer back to books that you've read, you can get on the Internet and do some research, or you can use the built-in PowerPoint help system. In this chapter, you'll learn how to:

- Use the Ask a Question help window
- Display the animated Office Assistant
- Browse the help files
- Find help on the Web

Finding Quick Answers

A new feature in Office programs is the Ask a Question text box. When you don't know how to perform a task, type a question in the box. You can use a regular question format or you can type a few keywords. Here's a quick example of what happens when you ask PowerPoint for help.

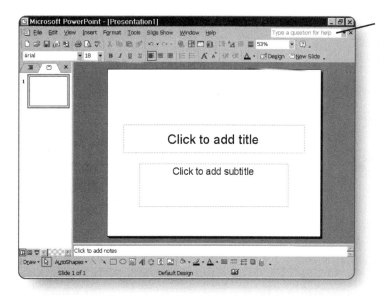

1. **Click** in the **Ask a Question text box**. The cursor will appear in the box.

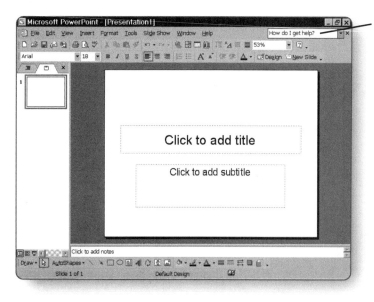

2. **Type** a **question** and **press Enter**. A list of help topics will appear.

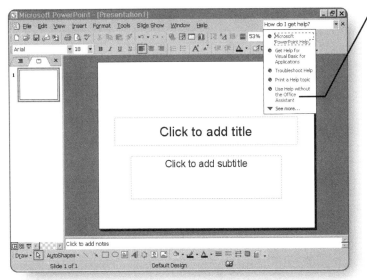

3. Click on the **topic** that most closely answers your question. The help topic will appear in the Microsoft PowerPoint Help window.

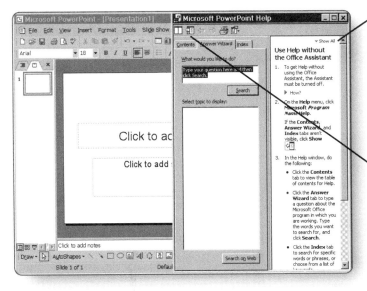

4. Click the **Show All hyperlink**. All of the instruction associated with the help file will also be displayed.

NOTE

Create more space by hiding the Index pane. Click on the Hide button.

5. Read the **help topic**.

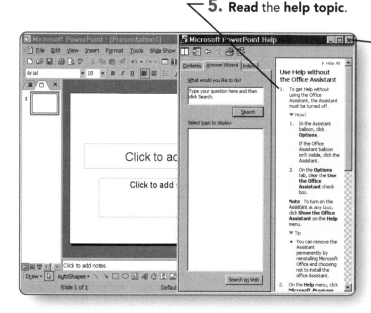

6. Click the **Close button**. The help window will disappear.

NOTE

You'll learn more about the Microsoft PowerPoint Help window later in this chapter.

Getting Help from the Office Assistant

Depending on how your installation of PowerPoint is set up, you may or may not see the Office Assistant on the screen.

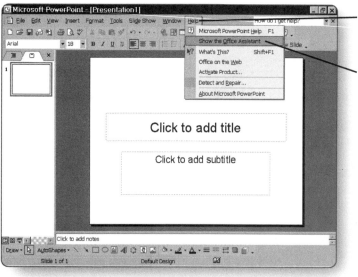

1. Click on **Help**. The Help menu will appear.

2. Click on **Show the Office Assistant**. An animated character will appear on the screen.

NOTE

This may be your last opportunity to hang out with Clippit. A recent layoff has forced Clippit to seek new opportunities. Visit Clippit at http://www.office clippy.com/indexno.html.

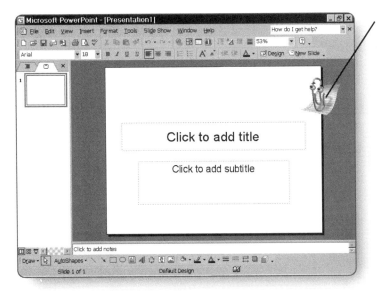

3. Click on the **Office Assistant**. The What would you like to do? message box will appear.

TIP

You can change to a different animated character if you get tired of looking at Clippit. Right-click on the Office Assistant and select Choose Assistant.

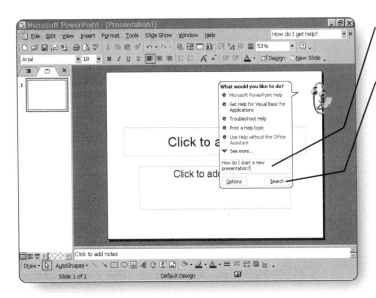

4. Type a **question** in the text box.

5. Click on **Search**. A list of possible help topics will appear.

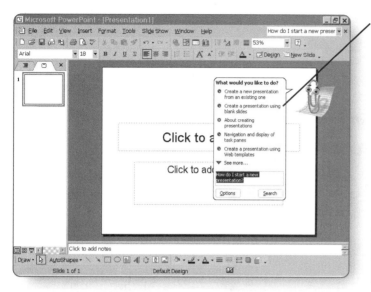

6. Click on the **topic** that most closely answers your question. The Microsoft PowerPoint Help window will appear.

TIP

Are you looking for a little entertainment? Right-click on the Office Assistant and choose Animate! from the Context menu. The Office Assistant will perform a trick for you.

---

7. Read the **help topic**.

NOTE

Click on the Print button if you want a paper copy of the help topic.

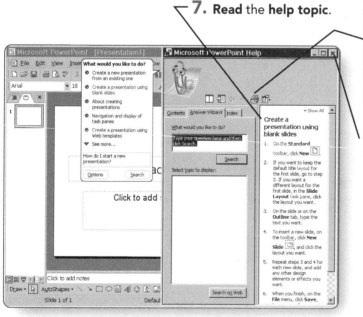

8. Click on the **Close button**. The help window will close.

Bypassing the Office Assistant

If you don't want to work with the Office Assistant, but you want to go directly to the PowerPoint help system, turn off the Office Assistant and then ask for help.

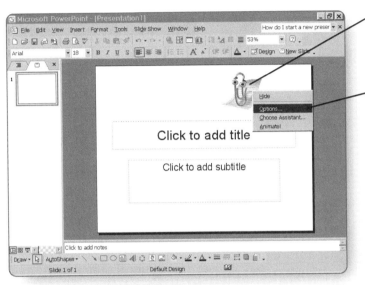

1. **Right-click** on the **Office Assistant**. A Context menu will appear.

2. **Click** on **Options**. The Office Assistant dialog box will open with the Options tab displayed.

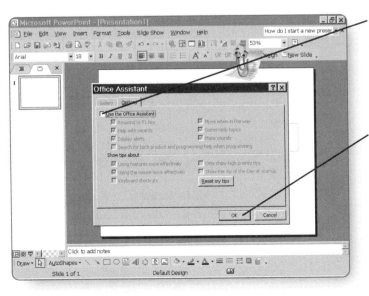

3. **Click** in the **Use the Office Assistant check box**. The check mark will be cleared and the Office Assistant options will be grayed out.

4. **Click** on **OK**. The Office Assistant will go away until you ask for it again.

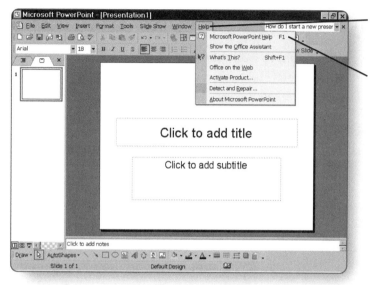

5. Click on **Help**. The Help menu will appear.

6. Click on **Microsoft PowerPoint Help**. The Microsoft PowerPoint Help window will appear.

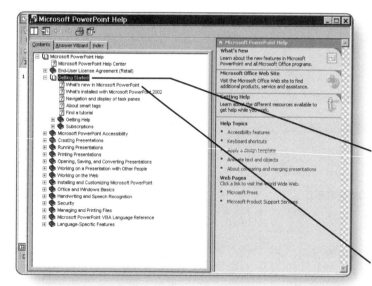

NOTE

If you do not see the list of help contents, click on the Contents tab.

7. Double-click on the **book icon** next to the subject you want to read about. The subject will expand and display a list of help topics.

8. Click on the **help topic** that you want to read. The help topic will appear in the pane on the right side of the window.

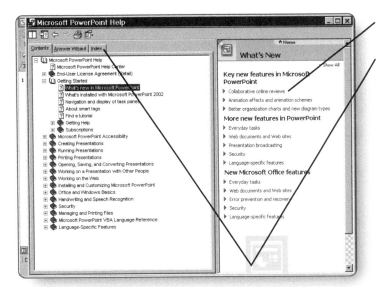

9. **Read** the **help topic**.

10. **Click** on the **Index tab** if you want to search the help topics for a keyword. The Index tab will come to the top of the stack.

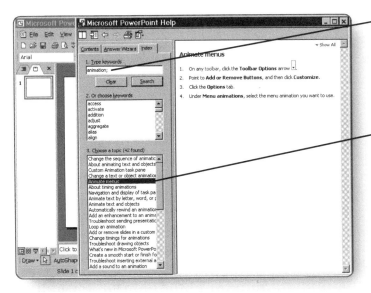

11. **Type** a **keyword** in the Type keywords text box and **press Enter**. The closest match will appear in the Choose a topic list box.

12. **Click** on a **topic** in the Choose a topic list box. The associated help file will appear in the pane to the right.

13. Use the **back and forward arrows**. You can scroll through help topics that you've recently read.

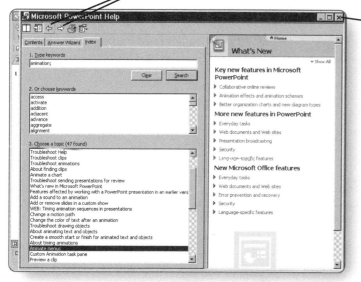

14. Click on the **Close button** when you are finished. The Microsoft PowerPoint Help window will close.

Visiting Office on the Web

When you want to keep up-to-date with the Microsoft Office products, visit the Office Update Web site. Before you can visit the Office Update Web site, you'll need an account with an Internet Service Provider and have a dial-up connection created on your computer.

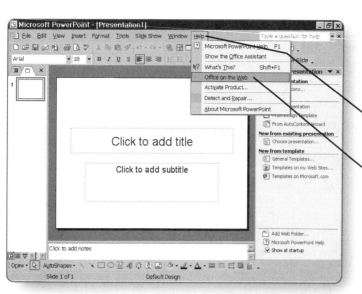

1. Click on **Help**. The Help menu will appear.

2. Click on **Office on the Web**. You will be connected to the Internet and your default Web browser will start.

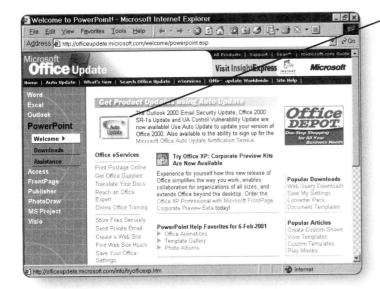

3. Explore the **Office Update Web site**.

3

Learning About Presentations

It's time to get started on your first presentation, but you don't know where to begin. Don't worry; PowerPoint contains a number of tools to help you take that first step. You'll find wizards and templates that help design professional looking presentations. You can use these wizards and templates as a learning tool or as a start for your presentation. In this chapter, you'll learn how to:

- Start a fast and easy presentation with the AutoContent Wizard
- Use templates to develop a uniform design
- Save a presentation
- Print a presentation

Using the AutoContent Wizard

PowerPoint contains two dozen presentations that can be used to get a quick start on a presentation. These presentations can be used to learn how an effective presentation is built or as a starting place for your own presentation. Each of these presentations can be changed to suit your needs.

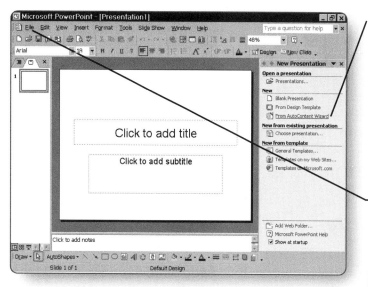

1. **Click** on **From AutoContent Wizard** in the New Presentation task pane. The AutoContent Wizard will start.

NOTE

If the Task Pane is not displayed, open the File menu and click on New. The New Presentation task pane will appear along the right side of the PowerPoint window.

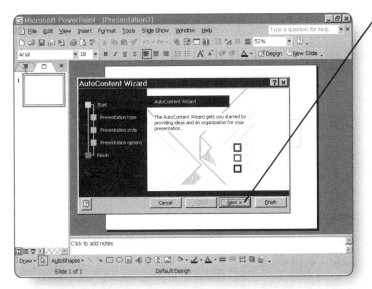

2. **Click** on **Next**. The Presentation type page of the wizard will appear.

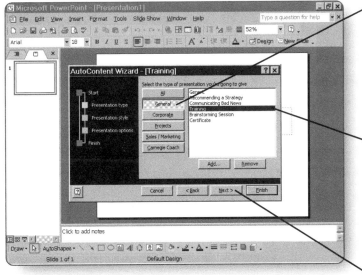

3. **Click** on the **button** for the category of presentation that you want to create. A list of presentation types will appear in the list on the right side of the dialog box.

4. **Click** on a **presentation type** that closely matches the information that you want to use in your presentation. The presentation type will be selected.

5. **Click** on **Next**. The Presentation style page of the wizard will appear.

6. Click on the **option button** for the method you will use to display the presentation. The option will be selected. Select from one of these options:

- An **On-screen presentation** is displayed on a computer monitor or on a projector connected to a computer. The computer must either have the PowerPoint program or the PowerPoint viewer installed.

- A **Web presentation** is one that is formatted in HTML and can contain hyperlinks and other Web page elements. This type of presentation can be viewed on the Internet or on a corporate intranet.

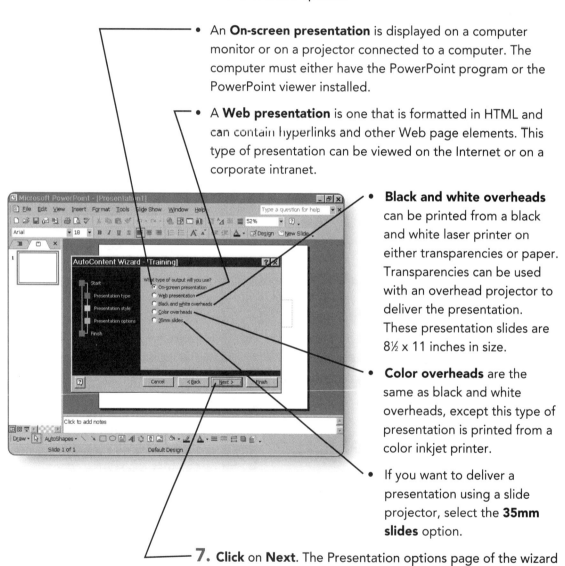

- **Black and white overheads** can be printed from a black and white laser printer on either transparencies or paper. Transparencies can be used with an overhead projector to deliver the presentation. These presentation slides are 8½ x 11 inches in size.

- **Color overheads** are the same as black and white overheads, except this type of presentation is printed from a color inkjet printer.

- If you want to deliver a presentation using a slide projector, select the **35mm slides** option.

7. Click on **Next**. The Presentation options page of the wizard will appear.

8. **Click** in the **Presentation title text box** and **type** a **title** for your presentation.

9. **Click** in the **Footer text box** and **type** the **text** that you want to appear in the footer area (found at the bottom of a slide) of each slide.

10. **Click** in the **Date last updated check box** if you do not want to display the last date on which you made updates to the presentation. This information is found in the footer area of a slide. The check box will be cleared.

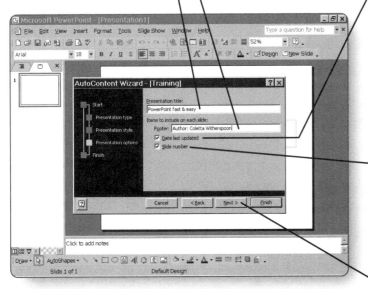

11. **Click** in the **Slide number check box** if you do not want to show the slide number in the footer area. The check box will be cleared.

12. **Click** on **Next**. The Finish page of the wizard will appear.

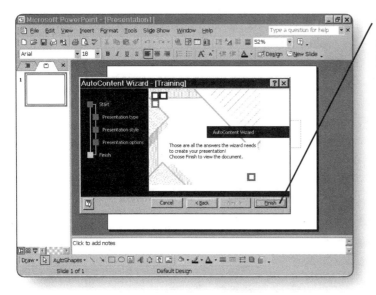

13. Click on **Finish**. The presentation will appear in the PowerPoint window.

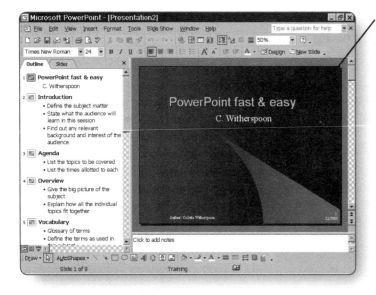

The AutoContent wizard creates a presentation that contains a starting point for an outline and a design template. You'll need to modify the outline to fit your presentation and the design template if you want to change the slide background and text font. You can also create a blank presentation and create your own design template.

Working with Design Templates

You don't need to be an artist to create a good-looking presentation complete with a background and other images. There are several design templates bundled in PowerPoint that will be pleasing to both you and your audience. Take a look at some of the design templates from which you can choose and see if any suit your needs.

Selecting a Template

If you don't have time to design a background and graphics for a presentation, try one of the design templates. Each design template uses text and images that work well together. Test some of the available templates and get some ideas on how you might customize your next presentation.

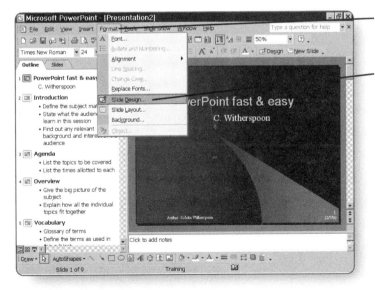

1. **Click** on **Format**. The Format menu will appear.

2. **Click** on **Slide Design**. The Task Pane will appear and thumbnails of the available design templates will be listed.

NOTE

There are more design templates than meet the eye. Use the scrollbar on the right side of the Task Pane to scroll through the list of design templates.

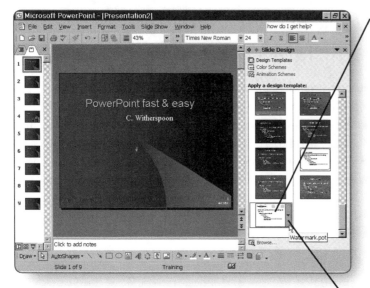

3. **Hold** the **mouse pointer** over a template that you want to use. A ScreenTip will appear showing the name of the design template. You'll also see a down arrow to the right of the template thumbnail.

4. **Click** on the **template** that you want to apply to your presentation. The template will be applied to every slide in your presentation.

TIP

You can apply a design template to selected slides in the presentation. First you must select the slides to which you want to apply the template. Then, click the down arrow to the right of the template and select Apply to Selected Slides.

Finding Templates on the Web

If, after looking through all the design templates, you still can't find one that you like, get on the Internet and see what's available.

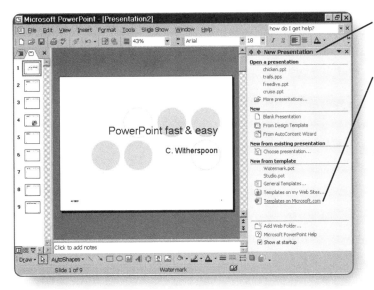

1. Display the **New Presentation task pane**.

2. Click on the **Templates on Microsoft.com link**. Your default browser will open and the Microsoft Office Template Gallery Home Page will appear.

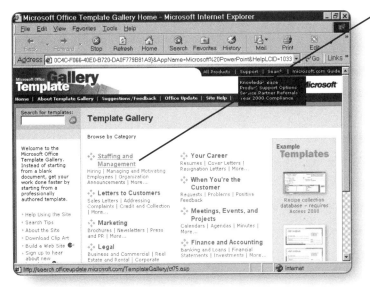

3. Click on a **category link**. A list of template types for that category will appear.

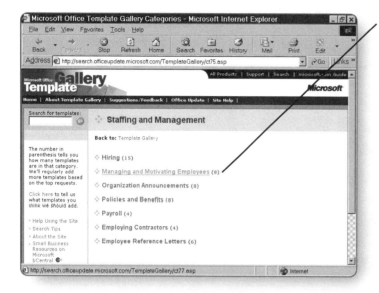

4. **Click** on a **template type**. Depending on the category that you chose, you may have to click through several lists. A list of templates will appear.

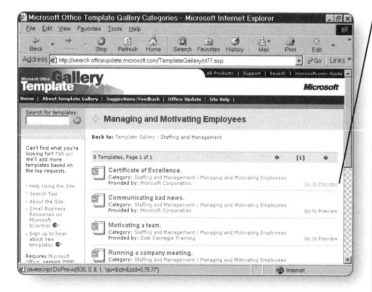

5. **Click** on the **Go to Preview link** for a PowerPoint template. The End-User License Agreement for Templates will appear.

NOTE

If the Microsoft Office Template Gallery ActiveX control is not installed on the computer, you will receive a Security Warning dialog box. Click Yes to download and install the ActiveX control.

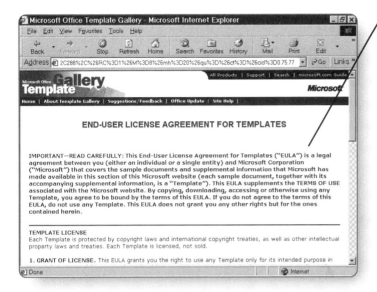

6. **Read** the **agreement**.

7. **Click** on the **Accept button**, which is found at the bottom of the Web page. The template will appear.

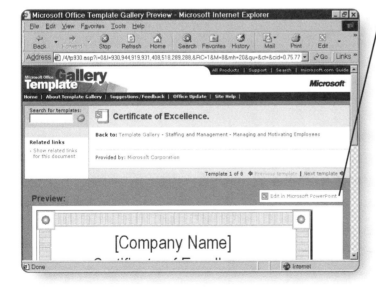

8. **Click** on the **Edit in Microsoft PowerPoint link**. The file will download to your computer.

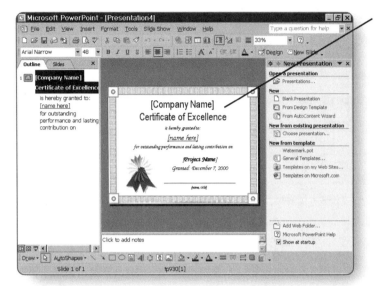

When the file has finished downloading, the presentation template will open in PowerPoint. You can then change the outline, edit the text, and select a different design template or color scheme.

Changing the Color Scheme

If you've found a design template that you like, but the colors aren't exactly perfect, change the colors of the different presentation elements. Before you begin, you'll need to click the back arrow on the Task Pane to return to the Slide Design task pane.

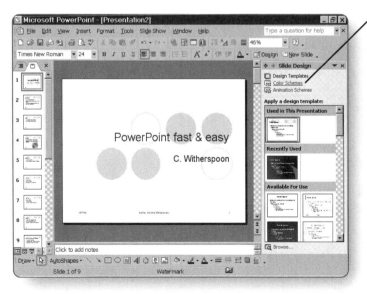

1. Click on the **Color Schemes link** in the Slide Design pane. A list of color schemes will appear.

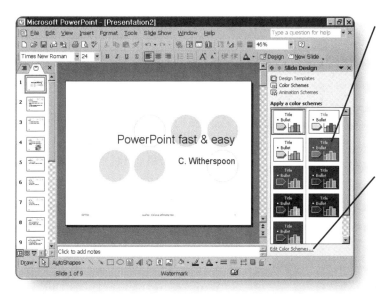

2. **Click** on the **color scheme** that you want to apply to the presentation. The color scheme will be selected and every slide in the presentation will be updated to match the color scheme.

3. **Click** on the **Edit Color Schemes link** if you want to change the color of individual slide elements. The Edit Color Scheme dialog box will appear and the Custom tab should be at the top of the stack.

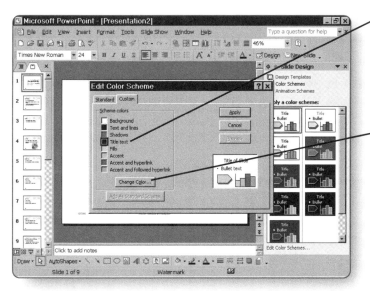

4. **Click** on the **color box** in the Scheme colors section for the elements that you want to change color. The color box will be selected.

5. **Click** on the **Change Color button**. The Color dialog box for the selected element will open.

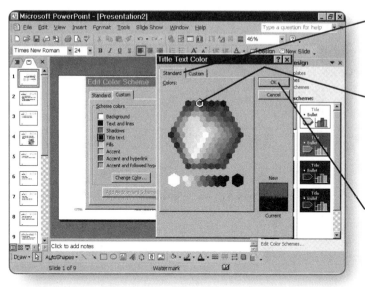

6. Click on the Standard tab. The Standard color options will display.

7. **Click** on the **color** that you want to apply to the element. The color will be selected and will appear in the New/Current preview area.

8. **Click** on **OK**. The Edit Color Scheme dialog box will appear and the color box for the selected element will change to reflect the color you selected.

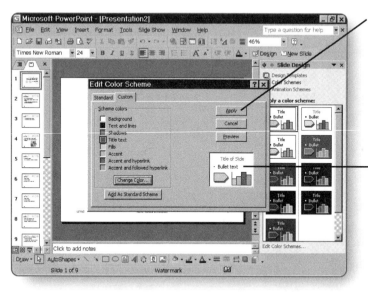

9. **Click** on **Apply**. The Edit Color Scheme dialog box will close and the new color scheme will be applied to the presentation.

NOTE

If you want to see the changes before you apply them to a presentation, look in the preview area of the dialog box. If you click the Preview button, the changes will be applied to your slides and the dialog box will remain open.

Working with Presentation Files

Before you get too involved in developing a presentation, you'll need to save the presentation file. Remember to save the file often so that you don't lose your valuable effort. Then, once you've started on the presentation, you'll want to see how you are progressing. You can easily preview the presentation or print it.

Saving Your Presentation

It can never be stressed enough that you must save your work and save it often while you are working on a presentation. Also, you may want to backup the presentation file to a floppy disk, a Zip disk, or a recordable CD in case you run into a computer problem.

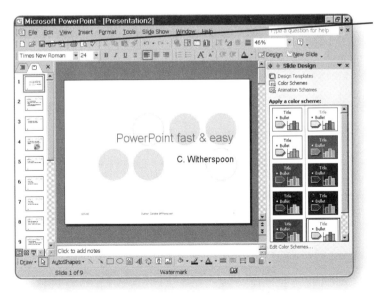

1. Click on the **Save button** on the Standard toolbar. The Save As dialog box will open.

2. Click on the Save in **drop-down list arrow** and **select** the **folder** in which you want to store the file. The folder will be selected.

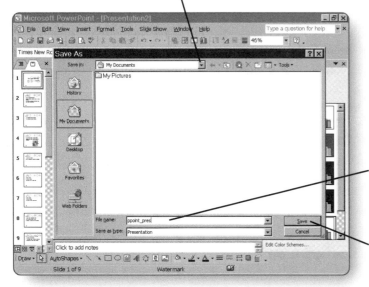

TIP

Some dialog boxes can be resized. Click and drag the resize handle found in the lower right corner.

3. Click in the **File name text box** and **type** a **name** for the presentation.

4. Click on **Save**. The presentation file will be stored in the designated folder and the file name will appear in the title bar of the PowerPoint window.

NOTE

After you've saved the presentation file the first time, you can save your changes by clicking on the Save button.

Previewing the Presentation

As you're working on a presentation, you may want to see how each slide looks before you print the presentation. Here's how to use the print preview feature to check your work.

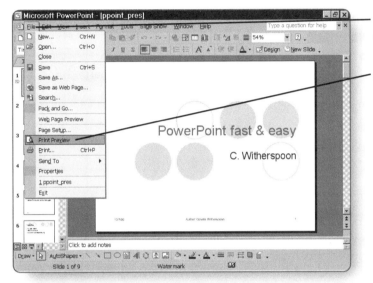

1. **Click** on **File**. The File menu will appear.

2. **Click** on **Print Preview**. The Preview window will appear.

3. **Click** the **Next Page button**. The next slide in the presentation will appear in the Preview window.

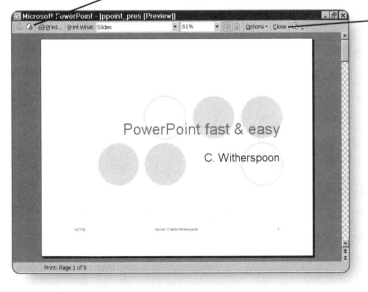

4. **Click** on the **Close button** to return to PowerPoint.

Printing the Presentation

When you want a paper copy of a presentation, send the file to a printer.

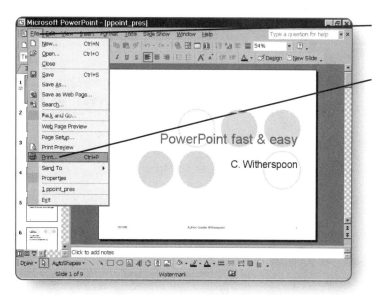

1. Click on **File**. The File menu will appear.

2. Click on **Print**. The Print dialog box will open.

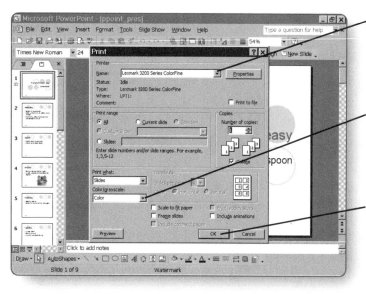

3. Click the **Printer Name drop-down list arrow** and **select** the **printer** to which you want to send the file.

4. Click the **Color/grayscale drop-down list arrow** and **select** the **color** in which you want to print the slides.

5. Click on **OK**. The presentation file will be sent to the printer.

Closing the Presentation

When you've finished working on a presentation, close the presentation file. You can close a presentation file without closing the PowerPoint program.

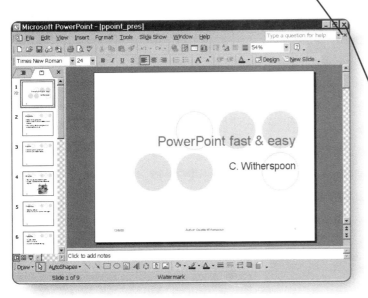

1. **Click** on the **Close button** for the presentation. The presentation file will close and PowerPoint will stay open.

2. **Click** on the **Close button** for the PowerPoint program. The program will close.

Opening a Saved Presentation

PowerPoint keeps a list of the saved files with which you've recently worked. This Recently used file list is found at the bottom of the File menu.

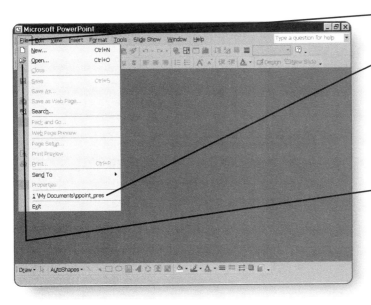

1. **Click** on **File**. The File menu will appear.

2. **Click** on the **presentation file** in the Recently used file list. The presentation will open in the PowerPoint window.

NOTE

If you don't see the presentation file in the list, click on the Open menu item to display the Open dialog box.

Part I Review Questions

1. What are the three different ways in which you can start the Microsoft PowerPoint application? See "Starting and Stopping PowerPoint" in Chapter 1.

2. Which PowerPoint view is used most often when designing the individual slides in a presentation? See "Looking at Your Viewing Options" in Chapter 1.

3. Name two tasks that can be accessed quickly by using the Task Pane. See "Working with the Task Pane" in Chapter 1.

4. Is it possible to resize dialog boxes in PowerPoint? See "Using Menus and Dialog Boxes" in Chapter 1.

5. What is the quickest way to find an answer to a question? See "Finding Quick Answers" in Chapter 2.

6. How do you print the information found in a Help topic window? See "Getting Help from the Office Assistant" in Chapter 2.

7. How do you turn off the Office Assistant? See "Bypassing the Office Assistant" in Chapter 2.

8. Where will you find existing presentations that you can edit to fit your needs? See "Using the AutoContent Wizard" in Chapter 3.

9. How do you change the colors used for text, graphics, and backgrounds? See "Working with Design Templates" in Chapter 3.

10. What types of media can you use to backup a presentation file? See "Working with Presentation Files" in Chapter 3.

PART II

Developing an Effective Presentation

4

Organizing the Presentation Outline

In the first part of this book, you learned how presentations work by looking at the presentation and design templates. You also learned how to use some of PowerPoint's features to design a presentation. Now it's time for you to fly on your own and start a presentation from scratch. In this chapter, you'll learn how to:

- Start with a blank presentation
- Develop a presentation outline
- Add text to a presentation and check your spelling
- Use a Microsoft Word outline in PowerPoint
- Print the outline

Starting with a Blank Presentation

If you don't want to use the predesigned PowerPoint templates, you can start with a blank presentation. From this blank presentation, you can design a presentation to fit your needs. You can design your own background and select colors, or you can use one of the design templates or color schemes.

1. **Click** on the **New button**. A blank presentation will appear in a separate PowerPoint window.

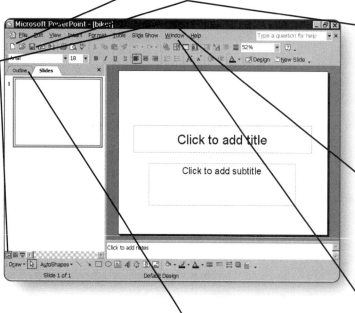

2. **Click** on the **Save button**. The Save As dialog box will open and you can specify the location and file name for the presentation. See Chapter 3, "Learning About Presentations," if you need help saving a file.

3. **Click** the **Normal View button**. The presentation will appear in the view in which you will perform most of your work.

4. **Click** on the **Outline tab**. The presentation outline will appear.

NOTE

You can switch between open PowerPoint presentation files from the Windows Taskbar or from the PowerPoint Window menu.

TIP

If you don't see this pane, open the View menu and select Normal (Restore Panes).

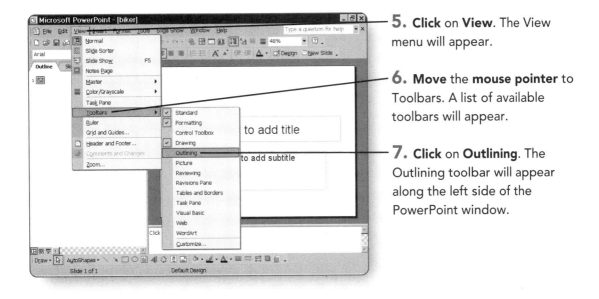

5. Click on **View**. The View menu will appear.

6. Move the **mouse pointer** to Toolbars. A list of available toolbars will appear.

7. Click on **Outlining**. The Outlining toolbar will appear along the left side of the PowerPoint window.

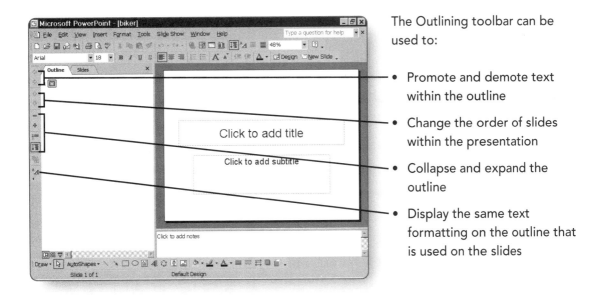

The Outlining toolbar can be used to:

• Promote and demote text within the outline

• Change the order of slides within the presentation

• Collapse and expand the outline

• Display the same text formatting on the outline that is used on the slides

Outlining the Presentation

The most important part of a presentation is the outline. The outline will keep your presentation organized and on track. Before you start adding graphics, animations, and transitions, make sure you have a solid foundation for your presentation.

> **NOTE**
>
> If you've created an outline in Microsoft Word, you can import that outline. To learn how, see the section titled "Sharing Outlines with Microsoft Word," later in this chapter.

Adding Items to the Outline

If you used the AutoContent Wizard to start your presentation, an outline has already been started for you. It is a simple matter of editing the outline by changing a few words or adding a few new slides. If you started with a blank presentation, you'll need to create each new slide by adding items to the outline.

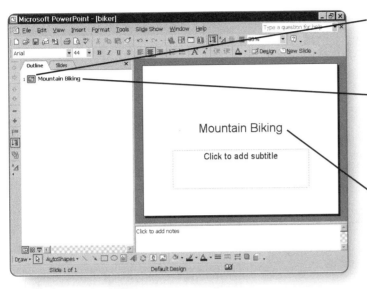

1. **Click** to the **right of the slide icon**. The insertion bar will appear.

2. **Type** the **text** that you want to appear as the title of the slide.

3. **Press** the **Enter key**. A new slide icon will appear and a blank slide template will appear.

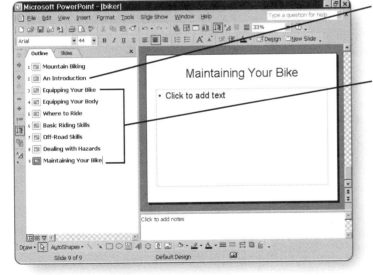

4. **Type** the **text** that you want to appear as the title of the second slide and **press Enter**.

5. **Continue adding text** until all the topics that you want to cover in the presentation appear in the outline.

Rearranging Items in the Outline

Once you've added the topics that you want to cover in the presentation, you may want to change the level at which some outline items appear. Here's where the Outlining toolbar comes into play.

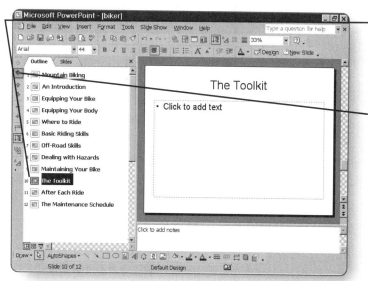

1. **Click** on the **outline item** that you want to demote to a lower outline level. The item will be selected.

2. **Click** on the **Demote button**. The text will be demoted to the next outline level.

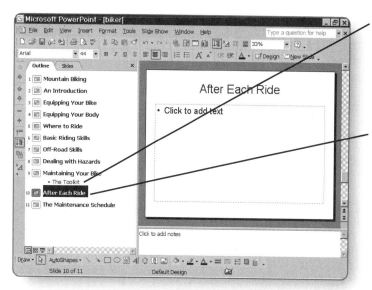

If the outline item was originally a first level heading (that is, a slide title), the text will become a bullet point and be contained in the slide that is above it.

3. **Demote other slides** as needed.

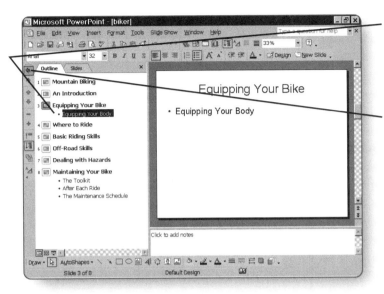

4. **Click** on the **outline item** that you want to promote to a higher outline level. The cursor will appear on the selected item.

5. **Click** on the **Promote button**. The text will be promoted. If the outline item was originally a bullet point, it will be promoted to a first level heading.

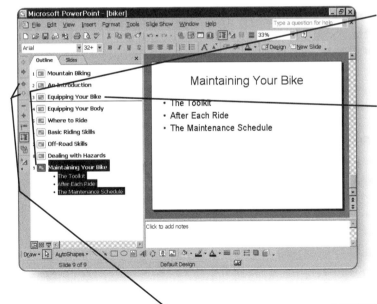

6. **Click and hold** the **slide icon** for the slide that you want to move. The slide icon and text will be selected.

7. **Move** the **mouse pointer** to the location where you want to place the slide. A line will appear to show where the slide will be inserted.

8. **Release** the **mouse button**. The slide and associated text will be moved to the new location.

NOTE
You can also move slides by using the Move Up and Move Down buttons on the Outlining toolbar.

Editing Text

Once the basic outline structure is in place, you can make any changes you want to the outline. You may need to change a few words or add a few new words.

Selecting Text

Before you can edit or format text, you'll need to select the text. Selected text appears inside a boxed background. The selected text can be a single letter or word, or several words. Here are a few tips for selecting text.

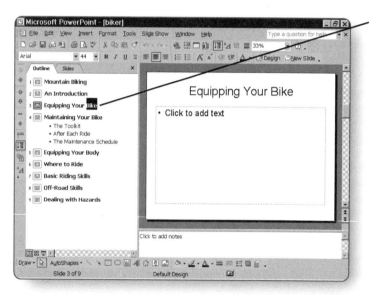

- To select a word, double-click on the word.

- To select an outline item, click three times on the item, or click on the slide icon on the Outline tab.

- To select the entire document, press Ctrl+A.

- To select a block of text, click and hold at the beginning of the text then drag the mouse pointer to the end of the text. Release the mouse button.

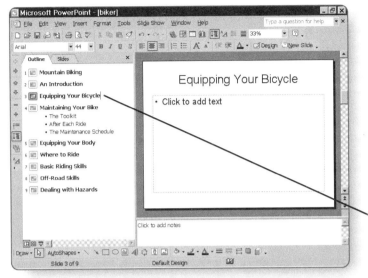

Replacing Text

When you need to revise items in the outline, select those words that you want to replace and add a few of your own.

1. **Select** the **text** that you want to replace. The text will be highlighted.

2. **Type** the **new text**. The selected text will be deleted and replaced with the new text.

TIP

Give your mouse finger a rest. Use the arrow keys to move around the outline. To select text, press and hold the Shift key while using the arrow keys to highlight the text.

Using Find and Replace

You can use the Find and Replace feature to search for text, such as individual words, phrases, or characters in a presentation. When you find this text, you can replace it with some other text, or you can delete it entirely.

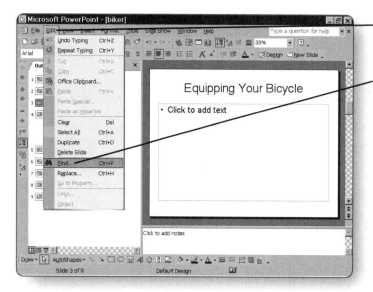

1. Click on **Edit**. The Edit menu will appear.

2. Click on **Find**. The Find dialog box will open.

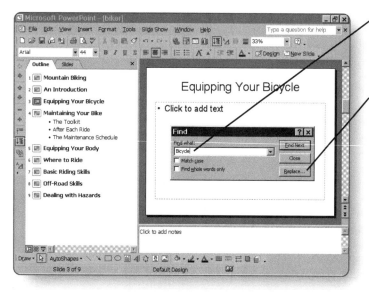

3. Type the **text** that you want to locate in the Find what text box.

4. Click on the **Replace button**. The dialog box will expand and display the area in which you type the replacement text.

5. Type the **text** to be used as the replacement in the Replace with text box.

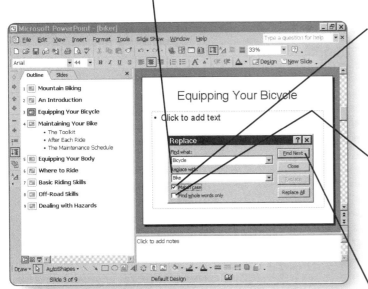

6. Click in the **Match case check box** if you want to find text that matches the upper- and lowercase letters you type. A check mark will appear in the check box.

7. Click in the **Find whole words only check box** if you want to match the exact words you typed in the Find what text box. A check mark will appear in the check box.

8. Click on the **Find Next button**. The first occurrence of the word(s) for which you are searching will be highlighted on the slide.

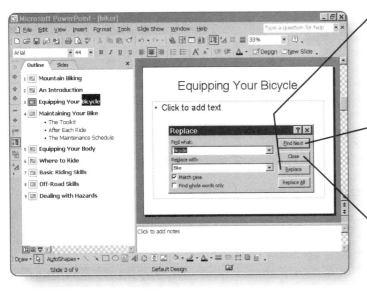

9. Click on **Replace**. The text that is highlighted on the slide will be replaced with the text specified in the Replace with text box.

10. Click on the **Find Next button**. The next occurrence of the specified word(s) will be highlighted on the slide.

11. Click on the **Close button** when you are finished replacing text. The dialog box will close and the changes will be made in the presentation.

NOTE

If you search the entire presentation, a dialog box appears that lets you know that PowerPoint has finished searching the presentation. Click OK to close this message box, and then click the Close button to close the Replace dialog box.

Spell Checking the Presentation

Before your presentation makes its debut, run the spell checker. Not only will the spell checker help you spot misspelled words, it will also tell you when you repeat yourself.

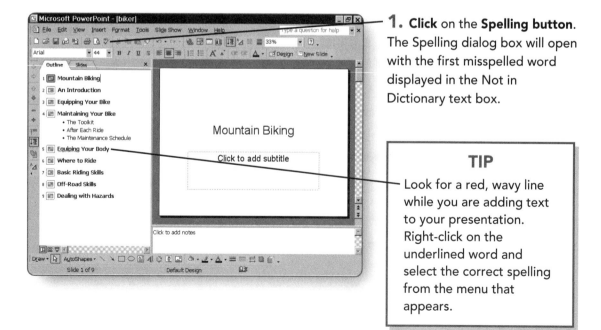

1. Click on the **Spelling button**. The Spelling dialog box will open with the first misspelled word displayed in the Not in Dictionary text box.

TIP

Look for a red, wavy line while you are adding text to your presentation. Right-click on the underlined word and select the correct spelling from the menu that appears.

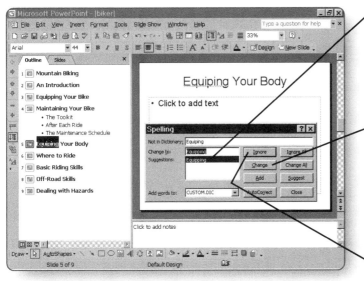

2. **Click** on the **correct spelling** in the Suggestions text box. The word will be selected and will appear in the Change to text box.

3a. **Click** on the **Change button**. The misspelled word will be corrected, and the next misspelled word will appear.

OR

3b. **Click** on the **Ignore button**. The word will be left as is and the next misspelled word will appear.

When PowerPoint has checked the last word in the presentation, a confirmation dialog box will appear.

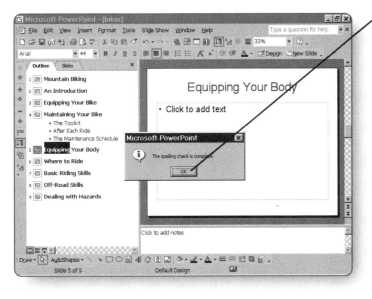

4. **Click** on **OK**. The presentation will be spell checked. You should save the file so that the corrections are preserved.

Sharing Outlines with Microsoft Word

If you use the outlining feature in Microsoft Word, you may find it easier to create the outline in Word and then import it into PowerPoint. If you started an outline in PowerPoint, you can export it into Word and edit the outline.

Importing an Outline

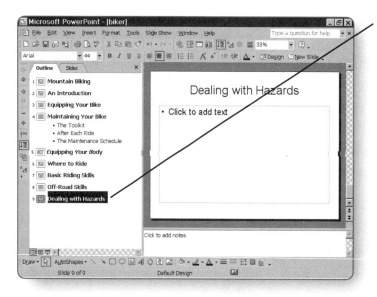

1. Click on the **slide icon** after which you want the Word outline to appear. The icon and slide text will be highlighted.

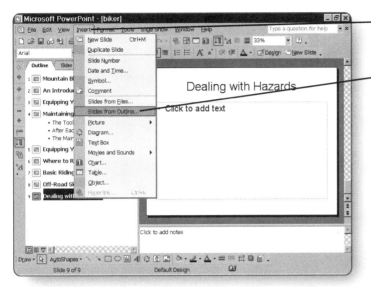

2. Click on **Insert**. The Insert menu will appear.

3. Click on **Slides from Outline**. The Insert Outline dialog box will appear.

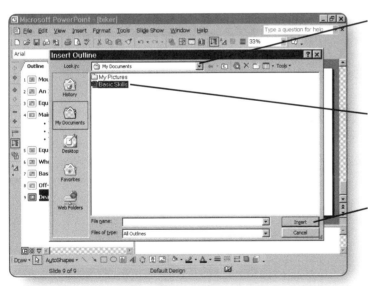

4. Display the **folder** in which you've stored the Word outline file. The folder will appear in the Look in list box.

5. Click on the **file** that contains the outline that you want to add to the presentation. The file will be selected.

6. Click on **Insert**. The outline will be inserted in the existing outline.

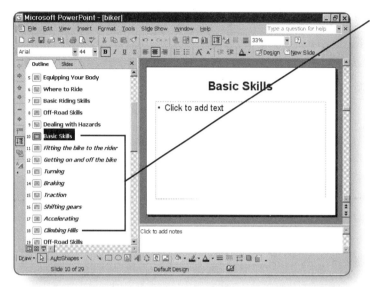

The first outline item from the imported file will be highlighted. You may need to promote and demote items in the outline. You can also move outline items around in the file.

Exporting an Outline

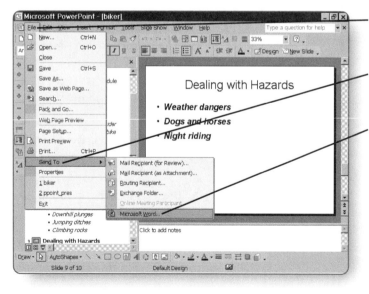

1. **Click** on **File**. The File menu will appear.

2. **Click** on **Send To**. The Send To submenu will appear.

3. **Click** on **Microsoft Word**. The Send To Microsoft Word dialog box will open.

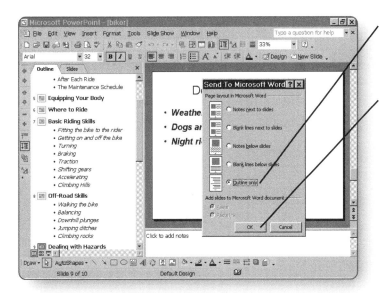

4. **Click** on the **Outline only option button**, if it is not already selected.

5. **Click** on **OK**. The outline will open in Microsoft Word.

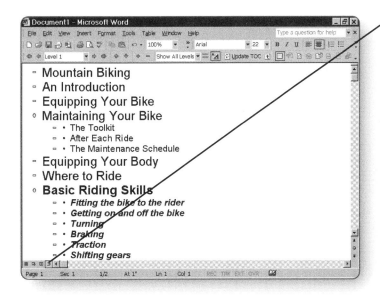

6. **Click** on the **Outline View button**. You can reorganize the outline using outlining features in Microsoft Word.

7. When you are finished with the outline in Word, save the file and close Word.

Printing the Outline

Before you print a presentation outline, display the items in the Outline tab that you want to print. If an item is collapsed (that is, hidden) it will not print. Use the Outlining toolbar to expand and collapse the outline.

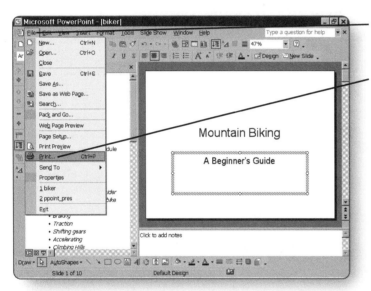

1. Click on **File**. The File menu will appear.

2. Click on **Print**. The Print dialog box will open.

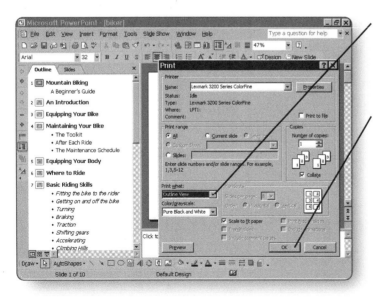

3. Click on the **Print what drop-down list arrow** and **select Outline View** from the list. The option will appear in the list box.

4. Click on **OK**. The outline will be sent to the printer.

5

Shaping Up Presentation Slides

Your presentation outline is finished and now it's time to work on the individual slides. You've got a lot of work ahead of you. There's still text to add to the slides, and you may think of places where you'll need to add more slides. Then, when you sit back and take a look, you just might find a few slides that would be put to better use if they were in a different location in the presentation. In this chapter, you'll learn how to:

- Use slide layouts to design individual slides
- Add words and sentences to slides and format the text
- Enhance the presentation by adding new slides and moving existing slides

Selecting a Slide Layout

When you created the outline, a slide was added for each first level heading. This heading is displayed in the title area of the slide. Subordinate text appears as bullet points under the title. There are other slide layouts that arrange bullet points in two columns or have a space in which you can insert a picture. Take a look through the list and decide which layout works best for an individual slide.

1. **Click** on the **slide** that you want to change. The slide will be selected.

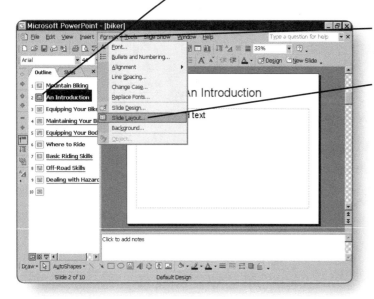

2. **Click** on **Format**. The Format menu will appear.

3. **Click** on **Slide Layout**. The Slide Layout task pane will open and the list of available slide layouts will be listed.

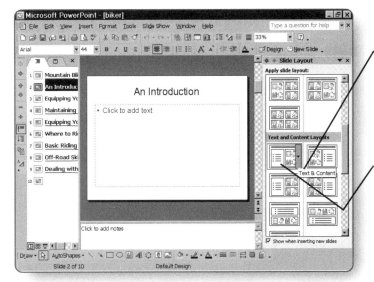

4. Click on the **layout** you want to apply to the slide. The slide will change to the new layout format.

Editing Slide Text

In Chapter 4, "Organizing the Presentation Outline," you learned how to work with text when creating a presentation outline. You also need to know how to work with text on the individual slides in the Normal view. Each slide in your presentation contains text that was created when you developed the presentation outline.

Adding Text

If you created an outline with first level headings only, you'll notice that the body of the slide contains a placeholder where you can add text.

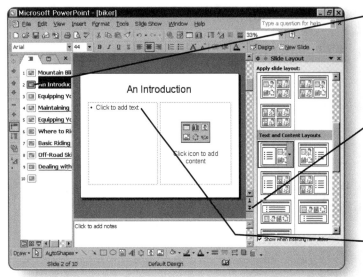

1. **Display** a **slide** that contains a text placeholder. The slide will appear in Normal view.

NOTE

To move from one slide to another in Normal view, click on the Next Slide button.

2. **Click** on the **text** in the placeholder. The placeholder text will disappear and the cursor will appear in the text box.

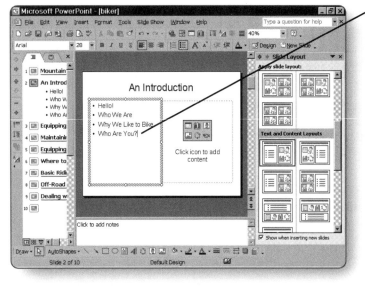

3. **Type** the **text** that you want to appear in the placeholder.

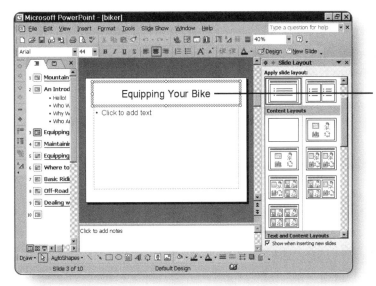

Here are a few of the text placeholders that you may run across:

- The **title placeholder** appears at the top of a slide. Use this placeholder to add text that describes the rest of the slide content.

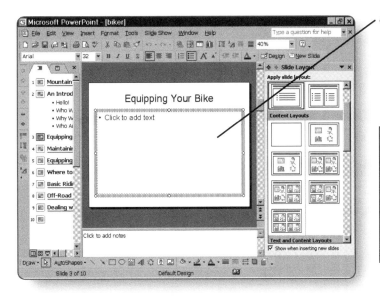

- A **text placeholder** can appear anywhere on a slide and will fit several lines of text. The default text is formatted as a bullet list.

TIP

The bullets can be removed. Select the bullet items and click on the Bullets button on the Formatting toolbar.

Deleting Text

The process for deleting text from a slide is identical to deleting text from the presentation outline.

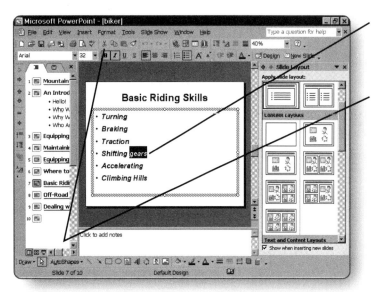

1. **Select** the **text** that you want to delete. The text will be highlighted.

2. **Click** on the **Cut button** or **press** the **Delete key**. The text will be removed from the slide.

Copying and Moving Text

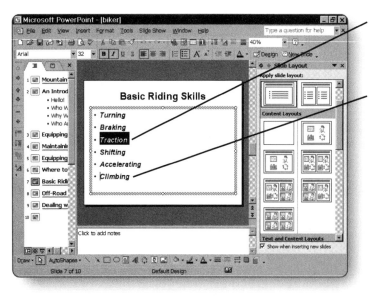

1. **Select** the **text** that you want to move or copy. The text will be highlighted.

2a. **Click** and **drag** the selected text to the place where you want it moved.

OR

2b. **Press** and **hold** the Control key to copy the selected text, and drag the selected text to the place where you want to put a copy of the text.

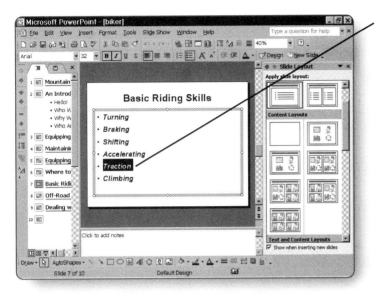

3. Release the **mouse button** when you are finished. The text will be moved or copied.

Formatting Slide Text

If you are using a slide design, the character and paragraph formatting contained in a presentation uses the design defaults. Sometimes, however, you may want to emphasize a word or group of words by using boldface, italics, or color. You may also want to change the font used on the presentation slides.

Working with the Formatting Toolbar

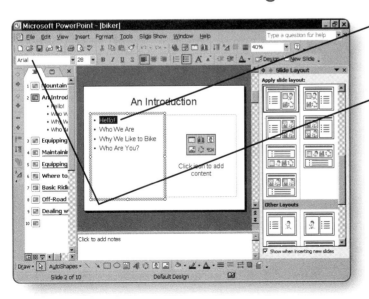

1. Select the **text** that you want to format. The text will be highlighted.

2. Click on a **Formatting toolbar button**. The text will be formatted in the style selected.

Here are a few formatting styles that you may want to apply to text:

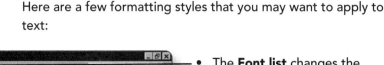

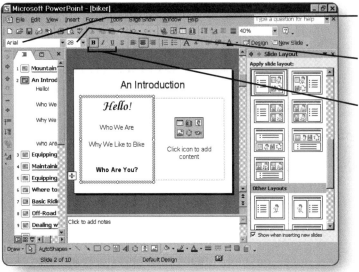

- The **Font list** changes the typeface used for the text.

- The **Font Size list** makes the text larger or smaller.

- Emphasize text so that it stands out from other text by using the **Bold**, **Italic**, and **Underline buttons**.

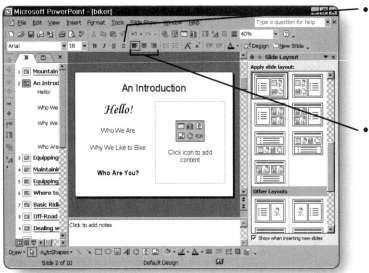

- The **Shadow button** should not be used on smaller text sizes or text contained inside a paragraph. It is best used as a special effect to enhance titles.

- By default, all placeholder text is left aligned. To change the way paragraphs appear on a slide, use the **Align Left**, **Center**, and **Align Right** buttons.

Copying Text Formatting

You can also copy the formatting of text and apply it to other text in a presentation slide:

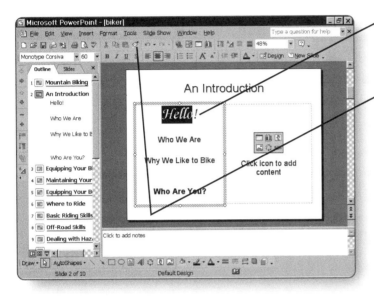

1. Select the **text** that is formatted in the style you want to format other text.

2. Click on the **Format Painter button** on the Standard toolbar. The mouse pointer will turn into a paintbrush.

> ### TIP
> Apply the copied formatting to more than one text element. Double-click on the Format Painter button. Press the Escape key when you are finished formatting.

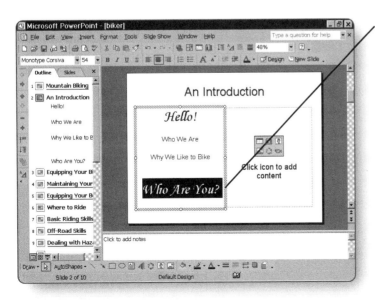

3. Select the **text** to which you want to apply the formatting.

Changing the Look of Bullet Lists

You may want to use a fancier bullet character than the plain dot used in bullet lists.

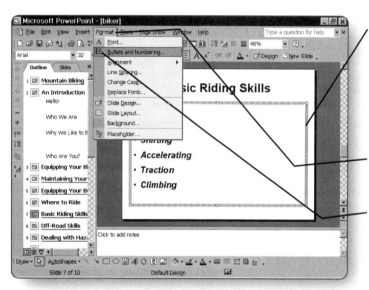

1. **Select** the **placeholder** that contains the bullet list. You'll need to click in a blank area inside the placeholder to select all the bullet items. The placeholder will be highlighted.

2. **Click** on **Format**. The Format menu will appear.

3. **Click** on **Bullets and Numbering**. The Bullets and Numbering dialog box will open.

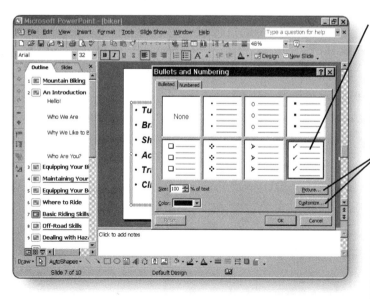

4. **Click** on the **bullet character** that you want to use for the bullet list. The bullet will be selected.

TIP

Use a custom bullet character. Click on the Customize button to select from a list of bullet characters. Click on the Picture button to select a colorful button or if you want to use a bullet that you designed yourself.

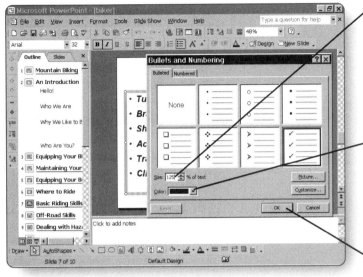

5. **Click** the **Size up and down arrows** to select how large or small the bullet will be compared to the text. The percentage you choose will appear in the list box.

6. **Click** the **Color down arrow** and **select** a color from the list. The color that displays in the list box will be applied to the bullet character.

7. **Click** on **OK**. The bullet character and color will be applied to all the bullet points in the placeholder.

Rearranging Slides

You don't have to work with just one slide at a time. The Slide Sorter view displays all the slides as miniatures in neat rows across the screen. This is a good way to see the "big picture" and view the progress of your presentation. Use this view to rearrange, add, and delete slides.

1. **Click** on the **Slide Sorter View button**. The presentation slides will appear in the Slide Sorter view.

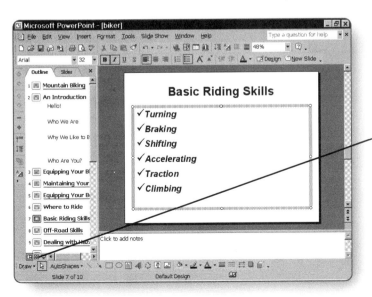

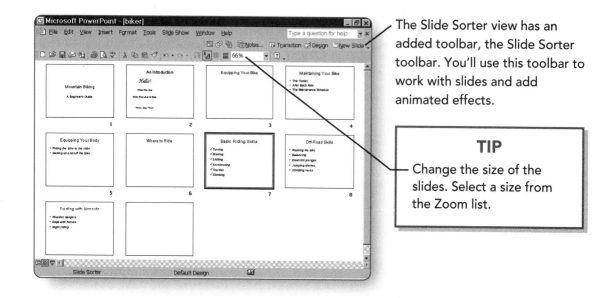

The Slide Sorter view has an added toolbar, the Slide Sorter toolbar. You'll use this toolbar to work with slides and add animated effects.

TIP

Change the size of the slides. Select a size from the Zoom list.

Selecting Slides

Before you can perform some functions with slides (such as deleting or moving), you'll need to select the slides with which you want to work. You can select a single slide, a contiguous group of slides, or random slides.

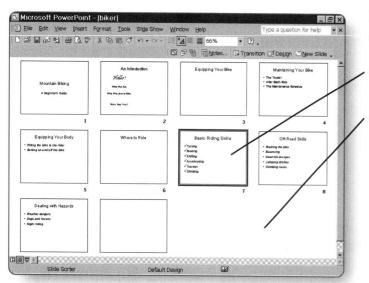

Here are a few tips for selecting slides:

- To select a single slide, **click** on the **slide**.

- To deselect a slide, **click** on a **blank area** of the Slide Sorter view.

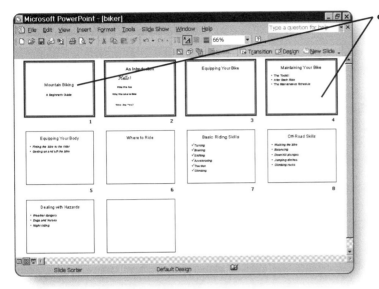

- To select a contiguous group of slides, **click** on the **first slide**, then **press** and **hold** the **Shift key** while clicking on the last slide in the group.

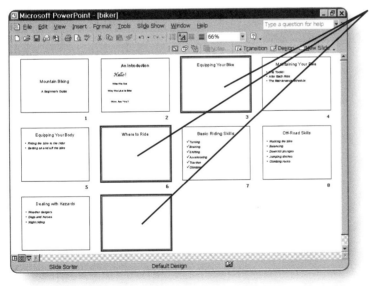

- To select random slides, **click** on the **first slide**, then **press** and **hold** the **Ctrl key** while clicking on the other slides you want to select.

Adding a Slide

While browsing in the Slide Sorter view, you may find a place where an extra slide is needed. You can easily add a new slide.

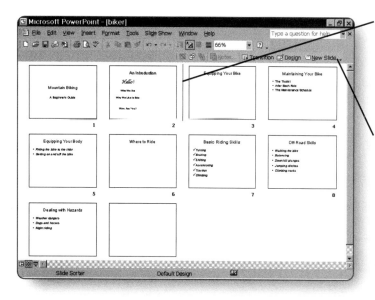

1. **Click** in the **space** between the two slides where you want the new slide to appear. The insertion bar will appear between the two slides.

2. **Click** on the **New Slide button** on the Slide Sorter toolbar. A new slide (using the default slide layout) will appear in the selected place. The new slide does not contain any text, but it does use the slide design that you have applied to the presentation. When you insert a new slide, the Slide Layout task pane also opens. You can select a layout from the list.

NOTE

To add text to the new slide, double-click on the slide to display it in Normal view.

Duplicating a Slide

When you want to make an exact copy of a slide, use the duplicate command.

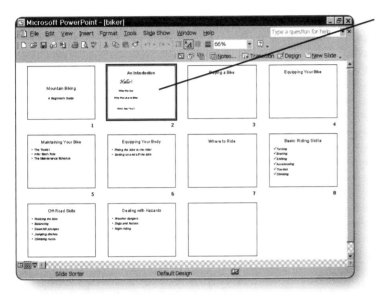

1. Click on the **slide** that you want to copy. The slide will be selected.

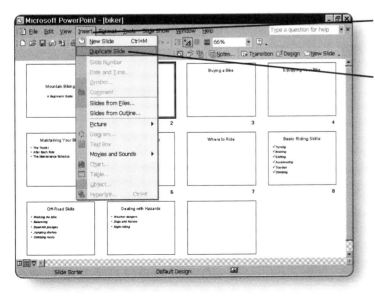

2. Click on **Insert**. The Insert menu will appear.

3. Click on **Duplicate Slide**. An identical slide will be created and will appear just after the original slide. The duplicate slide will be selected.

Moving a Slide

The Slide Sorter view can also be used to reorganize slides. Slides can be moved around to better present information with a simple drag and drop.

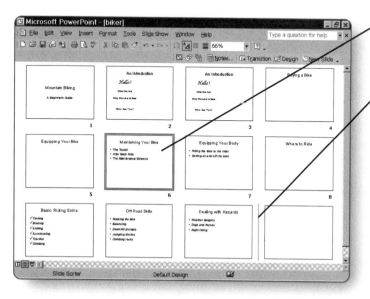

1. **Click** and **hold** on the **slide** that you want to move. The slide will be selected.

2. **Drag** the **mouse** to the place where you want the slide moved. The insertion bar will appear in the selected place.

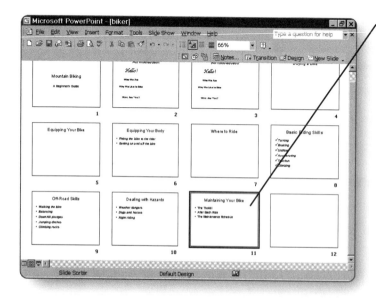

3. **Release** the **mouse button**. The slide will appear in the new position.

Deleting Slides

You may find that you don't need a slide in a presentation. Here is how to delete slides that you do not want.

1. Select the **slide or slides** that you want to delete. The slides will be selected.

2. Click on the **Cut button** on the Standard toolbar or **press** the **Delete key**. The slides will be removed from the presentation.

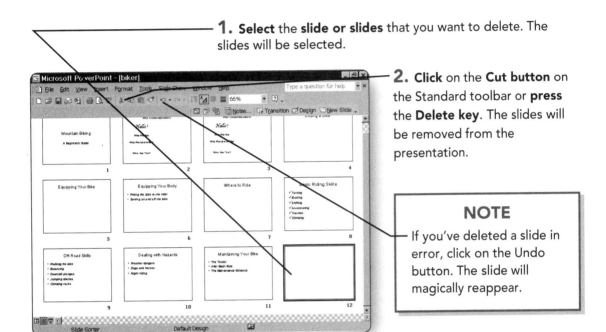

NOTE

If you've deleted a slide in error, click on the Undo button. The slide will magically reappear.

6

Customizing the Presentation

Does it seem like your presentation keeps growing and growing? Maybe other people have created a few slides to help you out and now you need to insert these into your presentation. And you may even need a few extra slides to help better organize your presentation. In this chapter, you'll learn how to:

- Add slides from one presentation into another presentation
- Use summary slides to help introduce major topics
- Apply a slide design to every slide in a presentation with a slide master

Inserting Slides from Another Presentation

If you have an existing presentation that you'd like to add to a presentation on which you are presently working, just insert the slides from the existing presentation. You can insert the entire presentation, or just a group of slides. Don't worry about any design templates that are applied to the existing presentation, they will take on the look of the presentation into which they are inserted.

1. Display the **presentation** in Slide Sorter view.

2. Click in the **space** where you want the slides from the other presentation to appear. The insertion bar will appear in the selected location.

3. Click on **Insert**. The Insert menu will appear.

4. Click on **Slides from Files**. The Slide Finder dialog box will open.

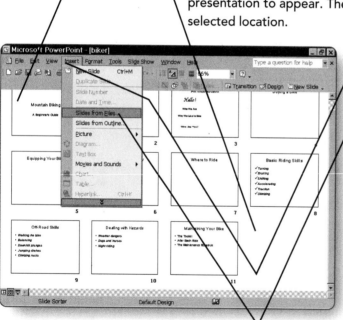

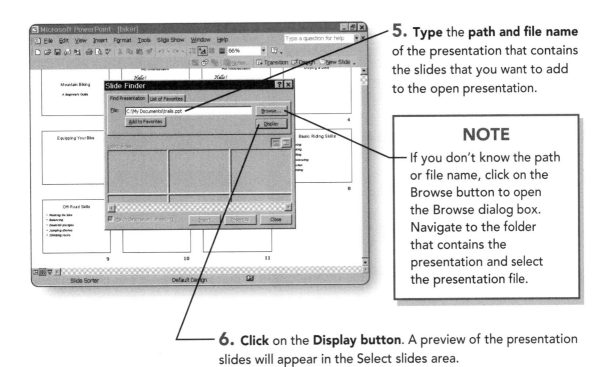

5. Type the **path and file name** of the presentation that contains the slides that you want to add to the open presentation.

NOTE

If you don't know the path or file name, click on the Browse button to open the Browse dialog box. Navigate to the folder that contains the presentation and select the presentation file.

6. Click on the **Display button**. A preview of the presentation slides will appear in the Select slides area.

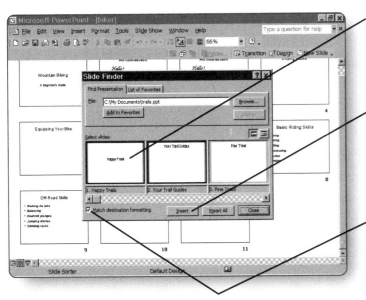

7. Click on those **slides** that you want to insert into the presentation. The slides will be selected.

8. Click on **Insert**. The selected slides will be inserted into the open presentation.

NOTE

If you want the slides to retain the original slide design, clear the Match destination formatting check box.

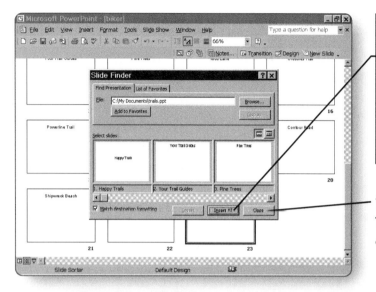

TIP

Use all of the slides from the presentation. Do not select any slides in the Select slides area. Click on the Insert All button to use all of the slides.

9. **Click** on the **Close button**. The Slide Finder dialog box will close.

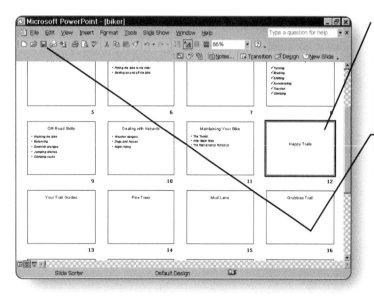

The slides from the existing presentation will appear in the selected position.

NOTE

Remember to save your work frequently.

Summarizing a Group of Slides

As you're working on a presentation, you may find places where it would help the presentation to have a slide that summarizes the main topics of a group of slides. You could create a separate slide to do this task, or you can save some time and let PowerPoint automate this task for you.

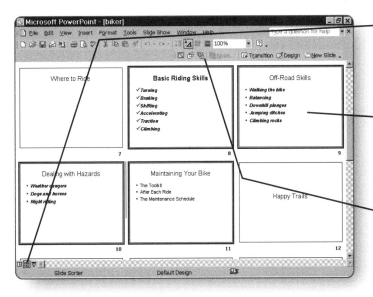

1. **Display** the **presentation** in Slide Sorter view. Miniatures of all the slides will appear on the screen.

2. **Select** the **slides** that you want to be listed on the summary slide. The slides will be selected.

3. **Click** on the **Summary Slide button** on the Slide Sorter toolbar. The summary slide will appear before the first selected slide.

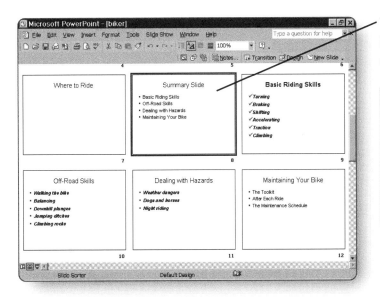

The summary slide contains a bullet list of the titles of the selected slides.

NOTE

You may want to change the title of the summary slide. Double-click on the summary slide to open it in Normal view.

Creating a Custom Slide Show

If you play a presentation for a variety of audiences, not all of the slides in your presentation may be suitable for every audience. A way to use a single presentation for different purposes is to create custom shows. A custom show is a show that only uses selected slides from the presentation. There are two types of custom shows, the basic custom show and the linked custom show.

Developing a Basic Custom Show

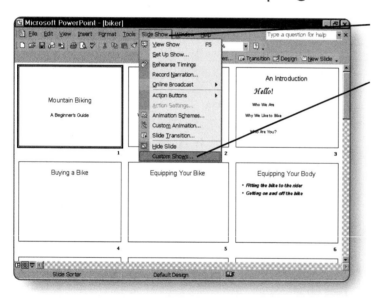

1. **Click** on **Slide Show**. The Slide Show menu will appear.

2. **Click** on **Custom Shows**. The Custom Shows dialog box will open.

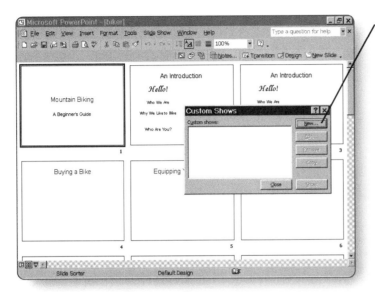

3. **Click** on the **New button**. The Define Custom Show dialog box will open.

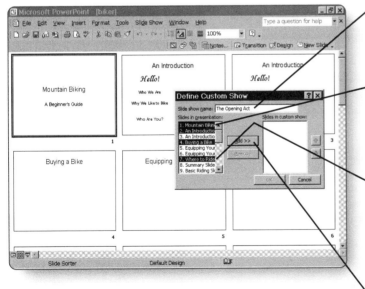

4. **Type** a **name** for the custom show in the Slide show name text box.

5. **Click** on a **slide** in the Slides in presentation list box that you want to include in the custom show. The slide will be selected.

6. **Press** and **hold** the **Ctrl key** while you click on the other slides that you want to include in the custom show. The slides will be selected.

7. **Click** on the **Add button**. The selected slides will appear in the Slides in custom show list box.

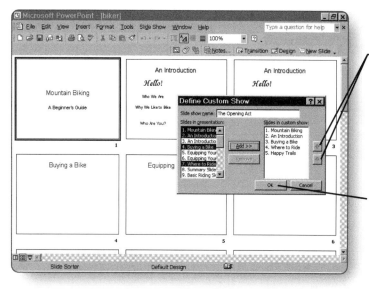

TIP

Change the order of the slides. Select a slide in the Slides in custom show list and use the up and down arrows to change the position.

8. Click on **OK**. You will be returned to the Custom Shows dialog box and the new custom show will appear in the Custom shows list box.

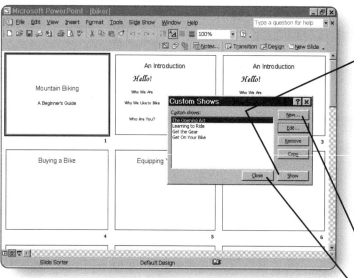

TIP

Preview a custom show. Select a custom show and click on the Show button. Use the arrow keys to move from slide to slide, and the Escape key to stop the preview and return to PowerPoint.

9. Create other **custom shows** if desired.

10. Click on the **Close button** when you are finished.

NOTE

You'll learn how to set up a presentation to run a custom show in Chapter 18, "Delivering the Presentation."

Linking to the Custom Shows

You may want to set up custom shows within a presentation so that all of the shows have a common introduction, and then use a summary slide to select from a list of custom shows. The summary slide uses hyperlinks to start a custom show. Before you begin, organize the slides into basic custom shows. Once this is done, create a summary slide that lists each custom show. And finally, create the hyperlinks that take you from the summary slide to the selected custom show and then back to the summary slide.

1. **Click** on the **Slide Sorter View button**. The presentation will appear in the Slide Sorter view.

2. **Select** the **first slide** from each of the custom shows. The slides will be selected.

3. **Click** on the **Summary Slide button** on the Slide Sorter toolbar. The summary slide will appear in front of the first selected slide. It contains a bullet list of the titles of the selected slides.

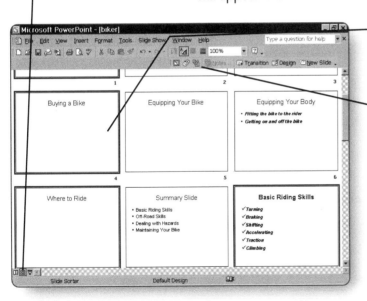

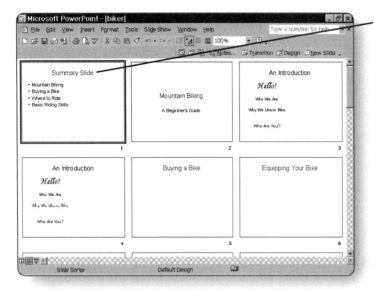

4. Double-click on the **summary slide**. The slide will open in Normal view and you can edit the text on the slide and create the hyperlinks.

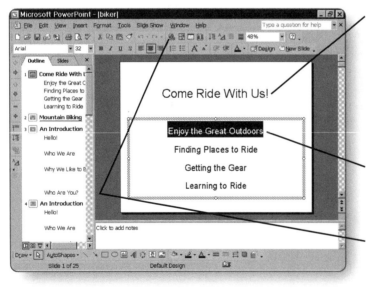

5. Select title and **bullet text** to change the title of the Summary slide and the text used for the bullet items. You may not want to use the same titles as the titles used on the first slide of each custom show.

6. Select the **first bullet list item**. The text will be highlighted.

7. Click on the **Insert Hyperlink button** on the Standard toolbar. The Insert Hyperlink dialog box will open.

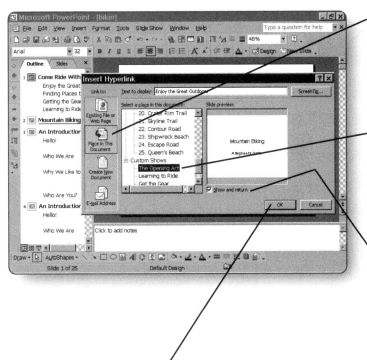

8. Click on the **Place in This Document icon** on the Places bar. The list of custom shows will appear in the Select a place in this document list box.

9. Click on the **custom show** to which you want to create the hyperlink. The first slide in the custom show will appear in the Slide preview area.

10. Place a **check mark** in the Show and return checkbox. When running a slide show, when you get to the end of a custom show you will be returned to the summary slide.

11. Click on **OK**. The hyperlink will be created.

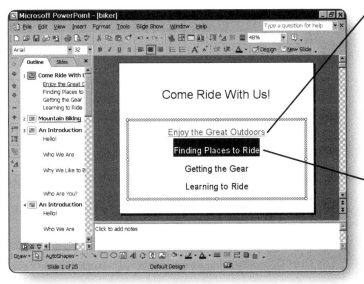

Notice that the hyperlink appears in a different color text and is underlined. If you want to learn more about using hyperlinks in PowerPoint presentations, turn to Chapter 19, "Publishing the Presentation on the Web."

12. Create hyperlinks for the remaining custom shows listed on the summary slide.

Designing a Slide Master

In Chapter 3, "Learning About Presentations," you saw how to apply a design template to all the slides in the presentation. The design template can be modified to suit your tastes. Or, if you elected to not use a design template, you can design your own look. These changes are made on the Slide Master. Think of the Slide Master as a style sheet that can be applied to every slide in a presentation.

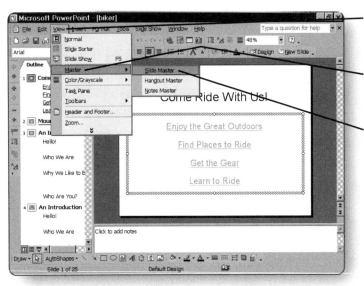

1. **Click** on **View**. The View menu will appear.

2. **Click** on **Master**. The Master submenu will appear.

3. **Click** on **Slide Master**. The Slide Master view will appear.

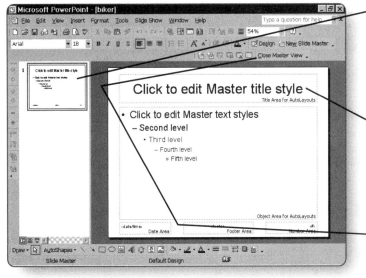

If you've applied a design template to a presentation, there are two Slide Masters. One is for the Title slide and the other is for all other slides.

4. **Make changes** as desired. Keep reading to find out some of the changes you can make. You are only limited by how creative and artistic you want to be.

5. **Click** on the **Close Master View button** when you have finished.

Changing the Slide Text

In Chapter 5, "Shaping Up Presentation Slides," you learned how to apply formatting to text on a single slide. You can also apply formatting styles to the master slides and they will appear on every slide. Before you begin, display the Slide Master using the steps above.

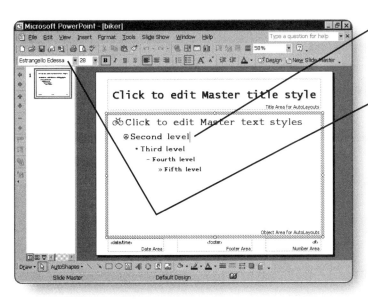

1. **Select** the **text** that you want to format. The text will be highlighted.

2. **Format** the **title style**, the **bullet levels**, and the **bullet characters** as you want.

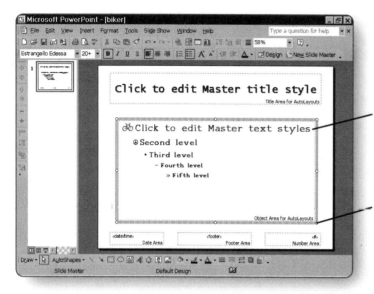

You can change the size of the Title Area, the Object Area, the Footer Area, the Date Area, and the Number Area placeholders.

3. **Click** on a **placeholder**. A border will appear around the placeholder that contains resize handles.

4. **Click** and **drag** a **resize handle**. A dotted line will appear to show the new size of the placeholder.

5. **Release** the **mouse button**. The placeholder will be resized. The slide text will be contained within the margins of the placeholder.

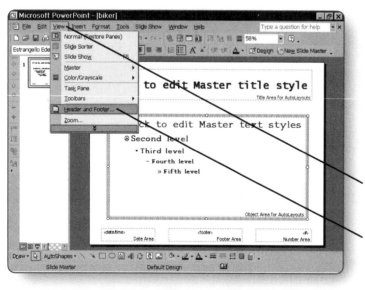

Adding Footers

There are several items that you can add along the bottom of each slide: the slide number, the current date, and any other miscellaneous text that you want.

1. **Click** on **View**. The View menu will appear.

2. **Click** on **Header and Footer**. The Header and Footer dialog box will open.

3. **Place** a **check mark** in the Date and time, Slide number, and Footer checkboxes if you want those items to appear in the footer area of each slide. A check mark will appear in the check boxes.

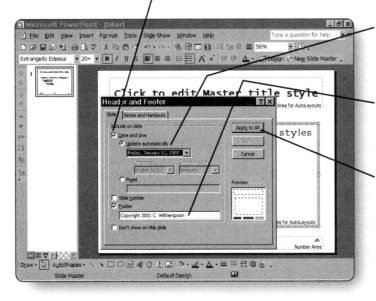

4. **Select Date** and **time options**. You can specify a date and time format.

5. **Type** other **text** that you want to appear in the footer area in the Footer text box.

6. **Click** on the **Apply to All button**. The footer information on the slide master will be updated.

Applying a Slide Background

You have hundreds of choices for a slide background. You can use clip art from the Microsoft Clip Organizer, clip art you found on the Internet, scanned photographs, or images you created in a graphics program, such as Microsoft Photo Editor. Explore your options.

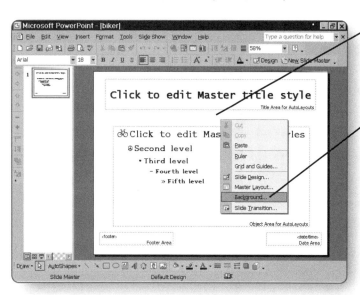

1. **Right-click** on an empty **area** of the slide master, outside of the placeholders. A context menu will appear.

2. **Click** on **Background**. The Background dialog box will open.

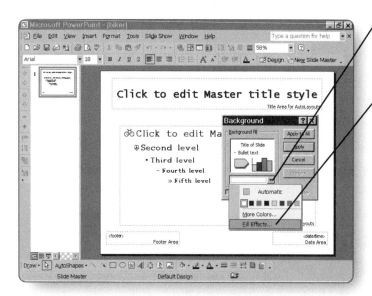

3. **Click** on the **Background fill down arrow**. A list of color options will appear.

4. **Click** on **Fill Effects**. The Fill Effects dialog box will open.

5. Experiment with **gradient backgrounds**, **textures**, **patterns**, and **pictures**. A preview of the background appears in the Sample area.

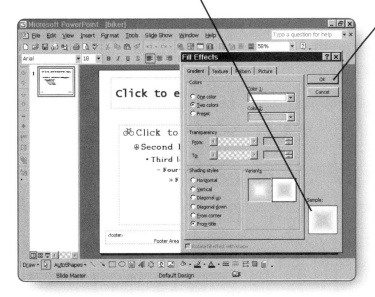

6. Click on **OK** when you have created a background. You'll be returned to the Background dialog box and you'll need to click on Apply to add the background to the slide master.

Part II Review Questions

1. Why should you use the Outlining feature to organize a presentation and how can the Outlining toolbar make this job easier? See "Starting with a Blank Presentation" in Chapter 4.

2. Which command would you use to replace several instances of one word with another word in a presentation? See "Using Find and Replace" in Chapter 4.

3. How do you use an outline created in Microsoft Word to help develop a PowerPoint outline? See "Sharing Outlines with Microsoft Word" in Chapter 4.

4. Where do you find templates to help you lay out the information on individual slides? See "Selecting a Slide Layout" in Chapter 5.

5. What is the easiest way to copy the formatting of a text element and apply it to other text on a slide? See "Formatting Slide Text" in Chapter 5.

6. How do you change the order in which slides appear in a slide show? See "Rearranging Slides" in Chapter 5.

7. When adding slides from another presentation, can you retain the original formatting of the added slides? See "Inserting Slides from Another Presentation" in Chapter 6.

8. What feature would you use to create a table of contents for a presentation? See "Summarizing a Group of Slides" in Chapter 6.

9. How do you break up a single slide show into several smaller slide shows? See "Creating a Custom Slide Show" in Chapter 6.

10. What is the easiest way to apply the same text formatting styles and background to every slide in a presentation? See "Designing a Slide Master" in Chapter 6.

PART III

Jazzing Up the Presentation

7

Inserting Graphics

You don't need to be a great illustrator to create slides with good-looking pictures. You just need to know how to work with the tools provided in PowerPoint. Myriad clip art images are at your disposal so that you can vary the design of your presentation. Change the color and size of clip art images to fit on the slide. Delete parts of an image if you want. Let your imagination have fun. You'll also find an arsenal of ready-made shapes and text effects that you can fill, color, and position anywhere. How creative do you want to be today? In this chapter, you'll learn how to:

- Browse the Clip Organizer for exciting graphics, photographs, sounds, animations, and video
- Use WordArt to enhance text on a slide
- Create line art images with AutoShapes

Working with Clip Art

The Microsoft Office programs use the clip art in the Clip Organizer. If you need picture ideas, browse through the Clip Organizer. Clip art is arranged by categories and can be searched by keyword or file type to help you find images faster.

Adding Clip Art

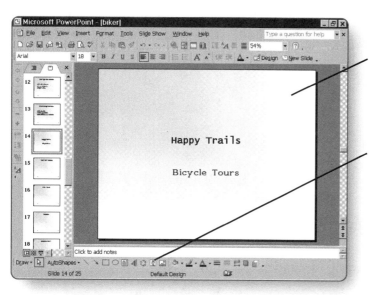

1. Display the **slide** to which you want to add the clip art image. The slide will appear in Normal view.

2. Click on the **Insert Clip Art button** on the Drawing toolbar. The Insert Clip Art task pane will open.

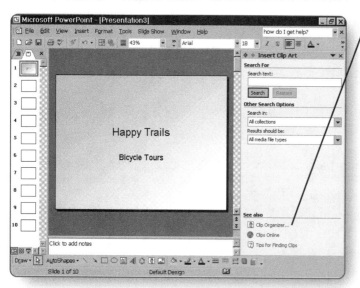

3. Click on the **Clip Organizer link**. The Microsoft Clip Organizer will open.

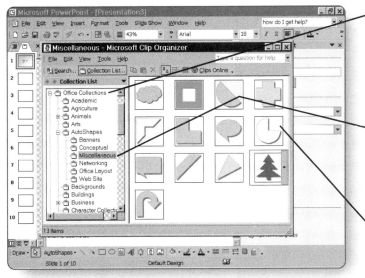

4. **Click** on the **plus sign** next to an item in the Collection List. The list of categories in the selected collection list will appear.

5. **Click** on a **category.** The clip art images contained in the category will appear in the right pane.

6. **Browse** through the list of images until you find one that fits your needs.

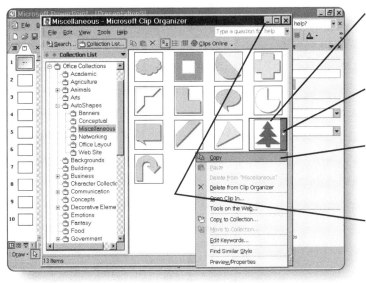

7. **Place** the mouse pointer over an image. A list arrow will appear at the right side of the image.

8. **Click** on the **list arrow**. A context menu will appear.

9. **Click** on **Copy**. The image will be copied to the Office Clipboard.

10. **Click** on the **Minimize button**. The Clip Organizer will become an icon on the Windows taskbar.

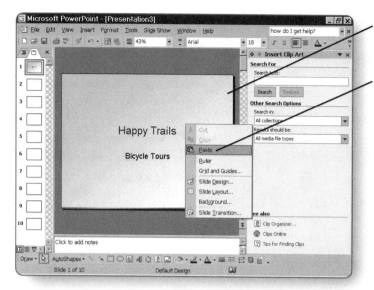

11. Right-click on the **slide**. A context menu will appear.

12. Click on **Paste**. The image will appear on the slide.

13. Resize the **image** to fit on the slide. Click and drag the resize handles.

Colorizing Clip Art

Once again, you have plenty of options for changing the look of clip art. When you click on a clip art image, the Picture toolbar should appear. If you don't see the Picture toolbar, display the View menu, move the mouse pointer to Toolbars, and select the Picture toolbar from the list. Experiment with the different options on the Picture toolbar and have some fun.

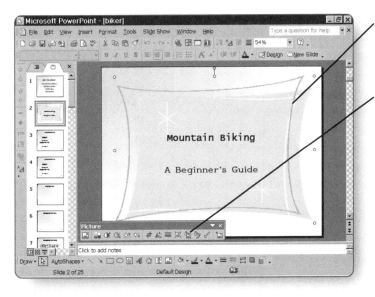

1. **Click** on the **clip art image** that you want to recolor. The image will be selected.

2. **Click** on the **Recolor Picture button** on the Picture toolbar. The Recolor Picture dialog box will open.

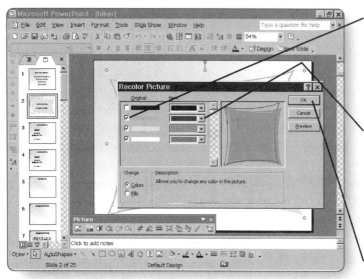

3. **Place** a **checkmark** in the checkbox next to the color that you want to change. A checkmark will appear in the check box.

4. **Click** the **New list arrow** and select a color to replace the original color. The new color will appear in the New list box and you'll see the changes in the preview area.

5. **Click** on **OK**. The picture will appear on the slide in the colors you selected.

6. Try out some of the other tools on the Picture toolbar:

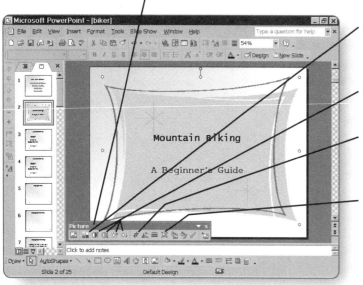

- Give clip art a faded look. Click on the Color button and select Washout.

- Change the brightness and contrast of an image.

- Eliminate unwanted edges of an image. Use the Crop button.

- Change the resolution and file size of an image from the Compress Pictures button.

Positioning Graphics on the Slide

It's not always easy to look at something (such as a picture hanging on a wall) and be able to line it up straight. That's when you need to break out the tools, such as a T-square, a level, or a ruler. You'll find all the tools you need to do the job in the PowerPoint toolbox.

> **TIP**
>
> If you are accustomed to using page layout programs, you may want to use grids and guides to help you position images. Click on the View menu and select Grid and Guides to get started.

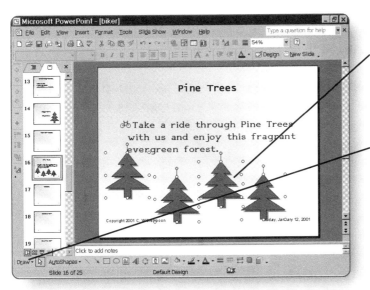

Aligning Graphics

1. Press and hold the **Shift key**, and click on the images that you want to align with each other. The images will be selected.

2. Click on the **Draw button** on the **Drawing toolbar.** A menu will appear.

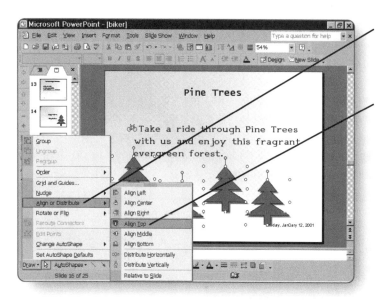

3. Move the mouse pointer to Align or Distribute. A second menu will appear.

4. Click on the **method** that you want to use to align the objects. The icon to the left of each menu command illustrates the type of alignment. The objects will be aligned relative to each other using the method you specified.

Grouping Graphics

1. Press and hold the **Shift key**, and **click** on the **images** that you want to combine to create a single image. The images will be selected.

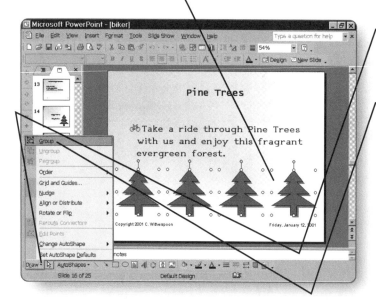

2. Click on the **Draw button** on the Drawing toolbar. A menu will appear.

3. Click on **Group**. The grouped images can now be treated as a single image.

TIP

If you want to ungroup, select the grouped object, click on the Draw button and select Ungroup.

Designing with WordArt

WordArt is another tool that you'll find in all Microsoft Office applications. WordArt is an easy way to create wavy and 3-D text effects. Here's another chance for you to play, but don't get too carried away. Overdone text effects can be a distraction and you don't want to lose a good audience.

Creating the WordArt Object

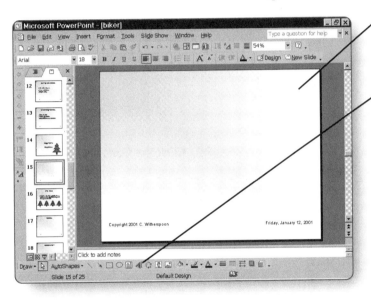

1. Display the **slide** that will contain the WordArt object. The slide will appear in Normal view.

2. Click on the **Insert WordArt button** on the Drawing toolbar. The WordArt Gallery dialog box will open.

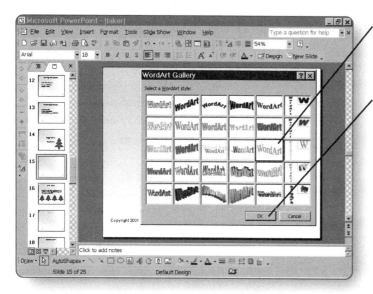

3. **Click** on the **WordArt style** that you want to use. The style will be selected.

4. **Click** on **OK**. The Edit WordArt Text dialog box will open.

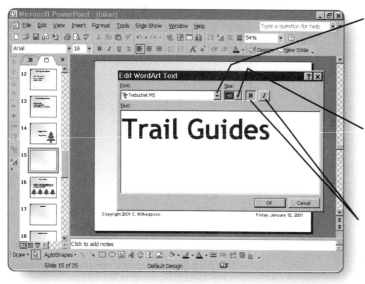

5. **Click** the **Font list box** arrow and select the font that you want to use in the WordArt object. The font name will appear in the Font list box.

6. **Click** the **Size list box arrow** and select the font size for the WordArt object. The font size will appear in the Size list box.

7. **Click** on the **Bold** or **Italic** **buttons** as desired to apply these styles to the text.

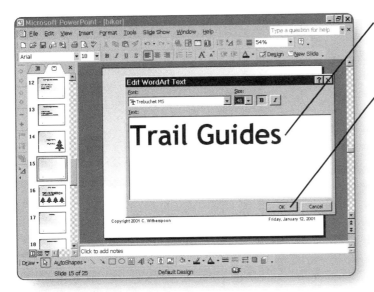

8. **Select** the **text** in the Text list box and **type** the **text** you want to appear in the WordArt object.

9. **Click** on **OK**. The dialog box will close and the WordArt object will appear on the slide.

10. **Click** on the **WordArt object**. The object will be selected and the WordArt toolbar will appear.

Customizing the WordArt Object

1. **Click and drag** a **resize handle**. The text size will change.

2. **Click and drag** the **rotate handle**. The object will turn in the direction you drag the mouse.

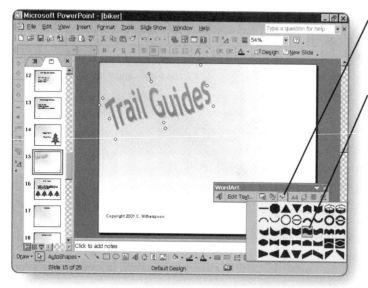

3. **Click** on the **WordArt Shape button** on the WordArt toolbar. A list of shapes will appear.

4. **Click** on a **shape**. The shape of the WordArt object will change.

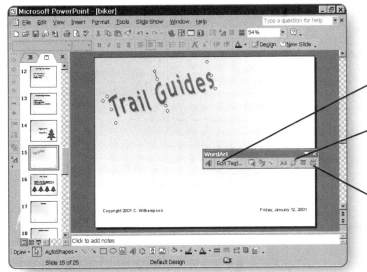

Here are some more editing tricks you can play on a WordArt object:

- Change the text by clicking on the Edit Text button.

- Stack letters on top of each other with the WordArt Vertical Text button.

- Change the spacing between characters with the WordArt Character Spacing button.

Adding Line Art

When you need a box, a circle, arrows, or callouts, you'll find a variety of ready-made styles from which to choose. When you're looking for banners and stars, or some irregular shapes, there's probably an AutoShape that can do the job. AutoShapes are easy to create: just a few mouse clicks and you have a shape you can adjust to fit your needs.

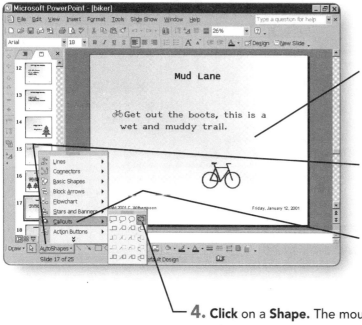

Creating a Basic Shape

1. Open the **slide** on which you want to insert the AutoShape. The slide will appear in Normal view.

2. Click on the **AutoShapes button**. A menu of AutoShape categories will appear.

3. Move the mouse pointer to a category. A list of shapes will appear.

4. Click on a **Shape.** The mouse pointer will turn into a crosshair.

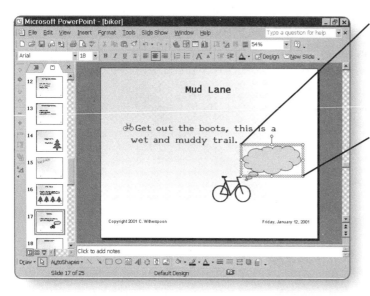

5. Click and drag the **mouse pointer** across the area on the slide where you want the AutoShape to appear. An outline will appear on the slide.

6. Release the **mouse button** when the shape is the desired size. The shape will appear on the slide.

Enhancing the AutoShape

You can change the color with which an AutoShape is filled, the color of the line that surrounds the shape, or the text contained inside a shape.

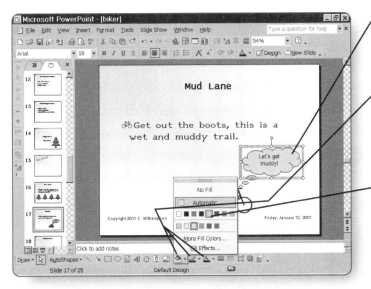

1. **Click** on the **AutoShape** that you want to change. The AutoShape will be selected.

2. **Click** on the **down arrow** next to the Fill Color, Line Color, or Font Color buttons. A menu of colors will appear.

3. **Select** a **color** from the menu. The color will be applied to the shape.

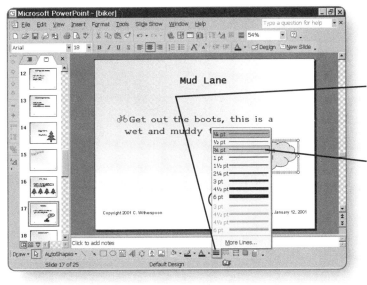

You can change the thickness of the line that surrounds the shape.

4. **Click** on the **Line Style button**. A menu of line choices will appear.

5. **Click** on the **style** that you want to apply to the shape. The line thickness of the shape will change.

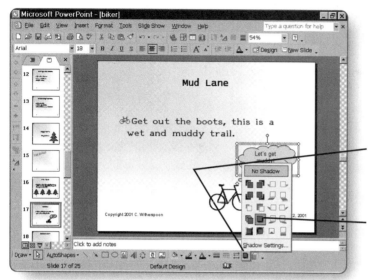

Sometimes, adding a shadow effect to a shape makes it appear to stand out from the slide. This is an easy way to make subtle enhancements that will attract the audience's eye.

6. Click on the **Shadow Style button**. A list of shadow styles will appear.

7. Click on a **shadow style**. The shadow will be applied to the shape.

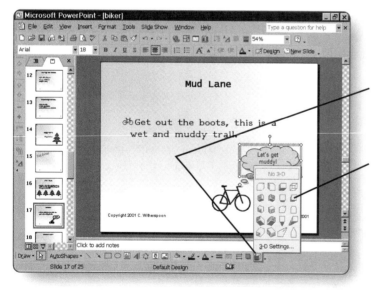

Some (but not all) shapes allow you to add 3-D effects to make shapes stand out from the slide.

8. Click on the **3-D Style button**. A menu of choices will appear.

9. Click on a **3-D style**. The style will be applied to the shape.

8

Using Digital Photographs

If you enjoy taking pictures and have a scanner attached to your computer, consider using your own photographs in your presentation. Before you begin scanning photos, set up the scanner and install the scanner software and the drivers necessary to operate the scanner. The scanner software may also come with photo editing software. Since each scanner comes with its own software, read the user manual carefully so that you can operate the scanner efficiently. Once this is accomplished, it's time to sort through the photo album and select a few pictures to scan. In this chapter, you'll learn how to:

- Scan photographs and place the images directly on a presentation slide
- Resize and crop images after they are inserted on a slide
- Do minor photo touch-ups such as adjusting the brightness and contrast
- Make a photo transparent or change it into a black and white photograph

Scanning Photographs

You can use PowerPoint to access scanner software to scan images and to make simple photo enhancements to the digitized image. Before you begin, make sure that the scanner software is installed and that you can use the scanner software to scan a photograph. PowerPoint can then access the scanner software, perform the scan, and then insert the scanned photograph on the presentation slide.

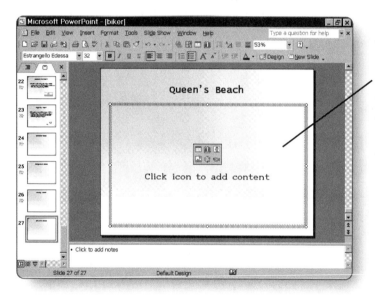

1. Position the **photograph** in the scanner.

2. Open the **page** where you want to insert the scanned photograph and place the cursor in the location where the image will appear.

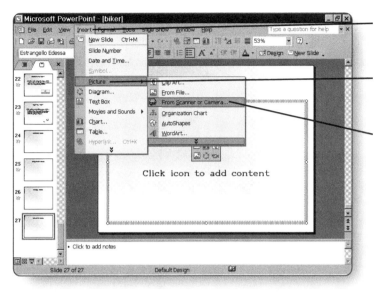

3. **Click** on **Insert**. The Insert menu will appear.

4. **Click** on **Picture**. The Picture menu will appear.

5. **Click** on **From Scanner or Camera**. The Insert Picture from Scanner or Camera dialog box will open.

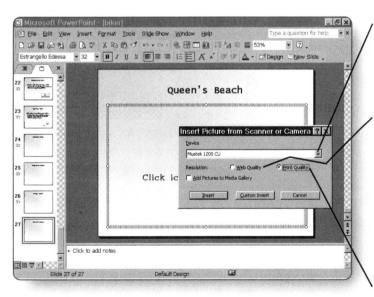

6. **Click** on the **Device drop-down list** and select the scanner from the list. The scanner name will appear in the list box.

7a. **Click** on the **Web Quality option button** if the presentation will be viewed over the Internet or on a computer screen. The option will be selected.

OR

7b. **Click** on the **Print Quality option button** if the presentation will be printed. The option will be selected.

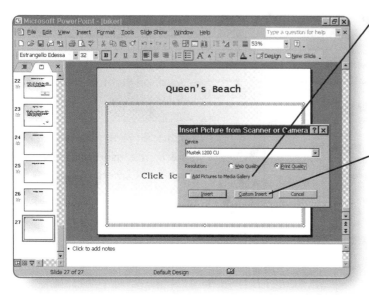

8. Click the **Add Pictures to Media Gallery check box** if you want to keep a copy of the photo in the Media Gallery. A check mark will appear in the check box.

9. Click on the **Custom Insert button**. The scanner software will start.

NOTE

Your scanning software will look different depending on the type of scanner you are using and the following steps may vary according to the scanner software.

---

10. Click on the **Preview button** in the scanning software. You may want to preview the photograph before you perform the actual scan. By previewing the scan, you can use the scanner software to make color adjustments and crop the image. A preview of the scanned photograph will appear in the scanner software window.

11. Make any **adjustments** in the scanning software as necessary.

12. Click on the **Scan button** in the scanning software. The scanner will digitize the image and place it on the slide.

NOTE

Some scanning software programs will close automatically once the scan is complete. If your software does not close automatically, either minimize or exit the program.

13. In PowerPoint, **click** on the **Save button**. The presentation file will be saved.

14. Click and **drag** the **resize handles**. The image will change size.

Enhancing Digital Photographs

After you've inserted a picture into a presentation slide, you may want the picture to look different. If you have simple image enhancements to make, you'll find a number of tools on the Picture toolbar.

1. **Click** on **View**. The View menu will appear.

2. **Click** on **Toolbars**. The Toolbars menu will appear.

3. **Click** on **Picture**. The Picture toolbar will appear.

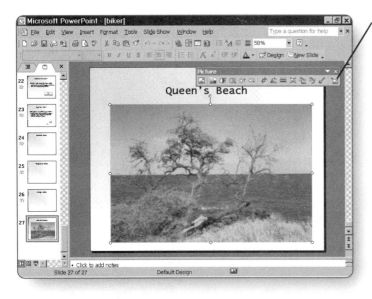

4. **Place** the **mouse pointer** over a Picture toolbar button. A ScreenTip that describes the button's function will appear.

Cropping Pictures

Unwanted edges of an image can easily be removed with the Crop button.

1. Click on the **Crop button** to display the crop marks.

2. Click and **drag** the **resize handles** until the part of the picture that you want to keep is inside the crop marks.

3. Click on the **Crop button** again to apply the changes to the image.

Rotating the Picture

There are two different ways to rotate a picture.

1. Click and **drag** the **rotate handle** to the right or to the left. The picture will turn as you move the mouse.

2. Click on the **Rotate Left button**. The picture will turn counterclockwise by 90 degrees.

Adjusting Brightness and Contrast

Sometimes all that's needed to make a picture look better is a little image enhancement trick. When an adjustment to the brightness or contrast is in order:

- **Click** on the **More Contrast button** to add definition between the light and dark colors in the image.

- **Use Less Contrast** to soften images that are too harsh.

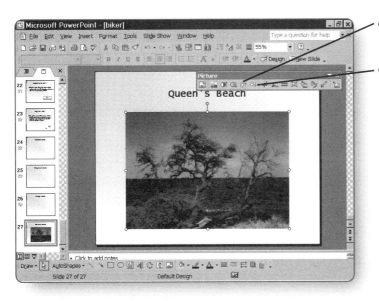

- **Select More Brightness** to lighten the colors in an image.

- **Try Less Brightness** to make an image appear darker.

Changing Colors

An easy way to change the look of an image is to change the color of the image.

1. Click on the **Color button**. A menu will appear.

2. Click on a **Color option**:

- To give images an old-fashioned, elegant look, use the Grayscale command.

- Give images a faded look by selecting Washout. The Washout command creates a light-colored, almost transparent, version of the image. The washout effect works well when you don't want an image to stand out on a page or if you want to place text over the image.

TIP

You can easily create an entire slide show that contains scanned photographs. To create a photo album presentation, click on Insert, Picture, New Photo Album. Just add photos and when you are finished, each photograph will appear on a separate slide.

9

Incorporating Tables

You've probably seen tables used in spreadsheets and word processing documents. Tables are a great way to organize information into neat rows and columns. Tables can be simple, or you can make them fashionable with designer lines and colors. In this chapter, you'll learn how to:

- Insert a table on a slide and add text to the table cells
- Change the size of the table, and of rows and columns within the table
- Create borders around the table and around individual cells in the table

Creating a Table

Before you begin building a table, you should have an approximate idea of the size you want. If you aren't exactly sure, you can always add and delete rows and columns later.

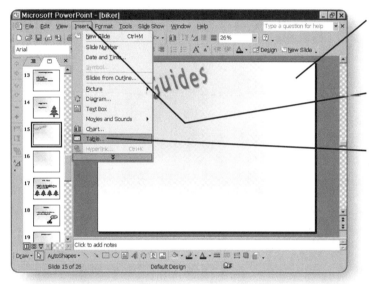

1. Open the **slide** on which you want to insert a table. The slide will appear in Normal view.

2. Click on **Insert**. The Insert menu will appear.

3. Click on **Table**. The Insert Table dialog box will appear.

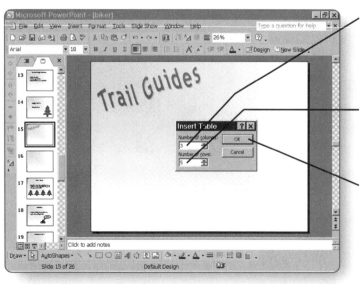

4. Click in the **Number of columns text box** and **type** the **number of columns** that should be contained in the table.

5. Click in the **Number of rows text box** and **type** the **number of rows** in the table.

6. Click on **OK**. The table will appear on the slide.

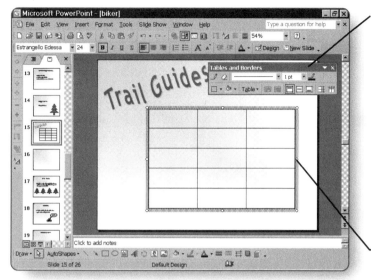

When you select the table, the Tables and Borders toolbar will appear. Use this toolbar to add rows and columns, create borders, and fill cells with color. If you don't see the Tables and Borders toolbar, right-click on an empty area of any toolbar and select Tables and Borders from the context menu.

TIP

Resize the table. Click and drag the resize handles to change the width and height of the table.

Inserting Text Into the Table

After creating the table, you can add words to the different cells. You can also format text in a table just as you would text on a slide.

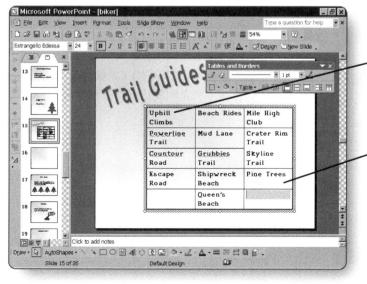

Adding Text

1. Click in the **cell** where you want to place the text. The insertion bar will appear in the cell.

2. Type the **text**. Several rows of text can appear in a single cell.

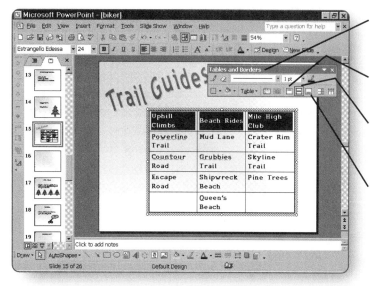

3. **Use** the **Tables and Borders toolbar** to align text in a cell.

- The Align Top button places text at the top of a cell.

- The Center Vertically button places the text in the middle of the cell.

- The Align Bottom button places text at the bottom of the cell.

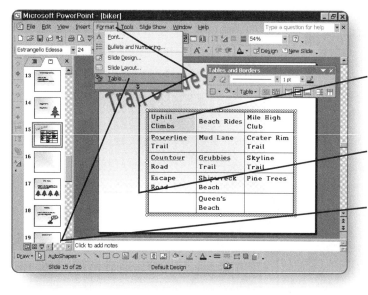

Changing Text Orientation

1. Click in the **cell** that contains the text to be rotated. The cell will be selected.

2. Click on **Format**. The Format menu will appear.

3. Click on **Table**. The Format Table dialog box will open.

4. **Click** on the **Text Box tab**. The Text Box options will appear.

5. **Click** in the **Rotate text within cell by 90 degrees check box**. A check mark will appear in the box.

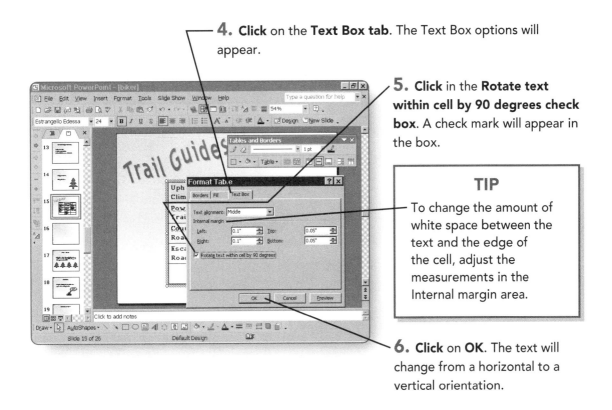

> **TIP**
>
> To change the amount of white space between the text and the edge of the cell, adjust the measurements in the Internal margin area.

6. **Click** on **OK**. The text will change from a horizontal to a vertical orientation.

Modifying the Table

If you find that a table doesn't contain enough cells, you may need to add a few rows or columns. Or, if you got carried away and have more table space than you need, start deleting extra cells.

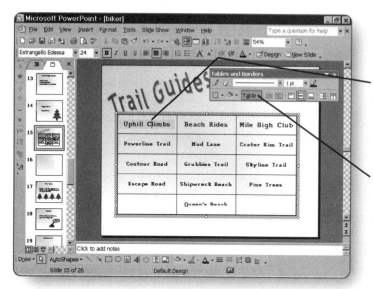

Adding Rows and Columns

1. Click in the **row or column** that will be adjacent to the new row. The insertion bar will appear in a cell.

2. Click on the **Table button** on the Tables and Borders toolbar. A menu will appear.

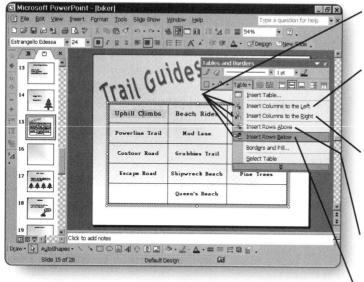

3. Select where to add rows and columns:

- **Click** on **Insert Columns to the Left** to place a new column to the left of the selected cell.

- **Click** on **Insert Columns to the Right** to place a new column to the right of the selected cell.

- **Click** on **Insert Rows Above** to place a new row above the selected cell.

- **Click** on **Insert Rows Below** to place a new row beneath the selected cell.

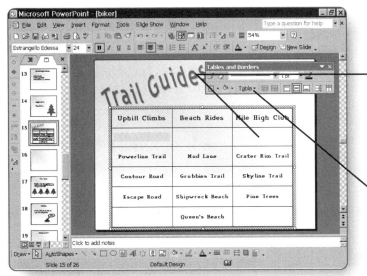

Deleting Rows and Columns

1. **Click** in a **cell** that is contained in the row or column that you want to delete. The insertion bar will appear in the cell.

2. **Click** on the **Table button**. A menu will appear.

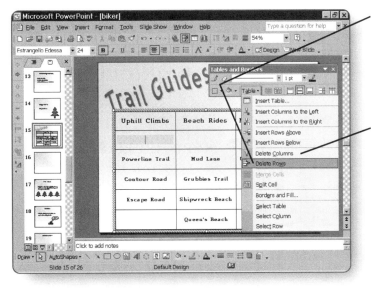

3a. **Click** on **Delete Rows**. The row in which the insertion point was positioned will be deleted.

OR

3b. **Click** on **Delete Columns**. The column in which the insertion point was positioned will be deleted.

Merging Cells and Splitting Cells

If you want to create a row across the top of the table in which to make a heading, you can combine several cells into a single cell. You can also split a cell into several cells to make space for additional information.

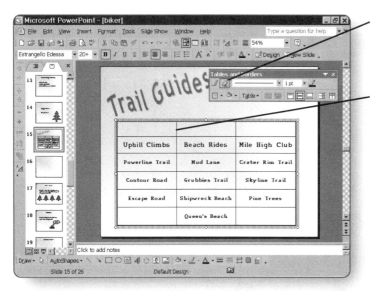

1. **Click** on the **Eraser button**. The mouse pointer will turn into an eraser.

2. **Click** on the **cell border** located between the two cells that you want to merge. The border between the two cells will be deleted.

3. **Click** on the **Eraser button** again when you are finished merging cells.

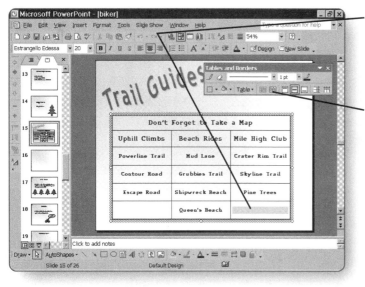

4. **Click** in the **cell** that you want to split into two cells. The insertion bar will appear in the cell.

5. **Click** on the **Split Cell button**. A new cell will be added to the table.

Resizing the Table

Sometimes tables need to be resized to fit on a slide or to display information in a neat and tidy format. Not only can you change the outer dimensions of a table, but rows may be made wider and cells taller.

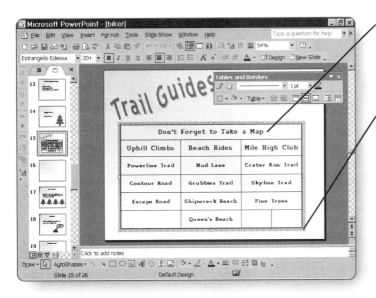

1. **Click** on the **table**. The table placeholder and the resize handles will appear around the outside border of the table.

2. **Click** and **drag** a **resize handle**. An outline of the table will show the new size of the table.

3. **Release** the **mouse button**. The table and all of the cells will be resized proportionately.

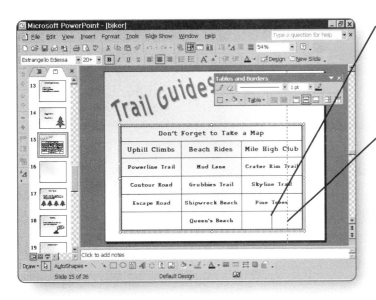

4. **Click** and **drag** on the **border** between two columns. The border will turn to an outline to show how the two columns will be resized.

5. **Release** the **mouse button**. The two columns will be different widths.

Formatting the Table

After you have created a table and added some text, you may decide that the table lacks color. Spruce up tables by adding background colors and by changing the color and style of the border lines.

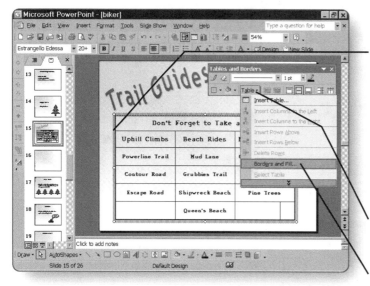

Designing a Border

1. **Select** the **table**. If you are not sure you have selected the entire table, click on the Table button and select Select Table from the menu. If the table is already selected, the Select Table command will be grayed out.

2. **Click** on the **Table button**. A menu will appear.

3. **Click** on **Borders and Fill**. The Format Table dialog box will open and the Borders tab will be displayed.

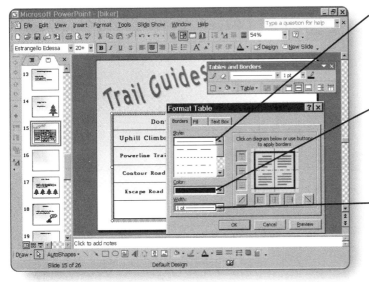

4. **Click** on the **line** in the Style list box that you want to apply to a border. The line style will be selected.

5. **Select** a **color** from the Color list box to apply to the line style. The color will appear in the list box.

6. **Select** a **line width** from the Width list box. The width will appear in the list box.

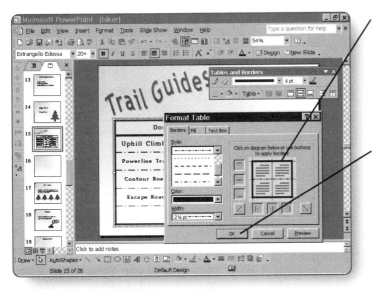

7. **Click** on the **border** in the diagram to which you want to apply the line style. The diagram will be updated with the new border line style. You will need to click once for each border.

8. **Click** on **OK** when you are done. The table border will be updated with the new line style format.

Adding Color to Cells

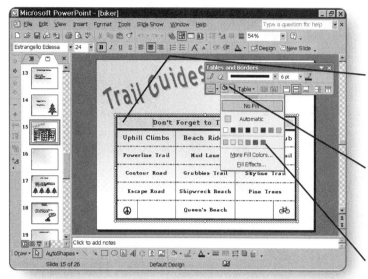

1. **Select** the **cells** to which you want to add a background fill color. The cells will be highlighted.

2. **Click** on the **down arrow** next to the Fill Color button. A list of colors from which you can choose will appear.

3. **Click** on a **Color**. The selected cells will be filled with the new color.

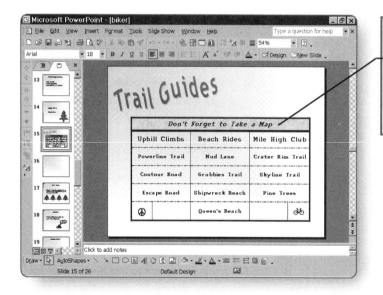

TIP

Try out the Fill Effects option on the Fill Color list to make some real fancy tables.

10

Producing Charts and Graphs

Charts and graphs are the visual representation of a relationship between two or more items. They can show a trend over a period of time or an item's size in relation to the total. All these relationships can be displayed with bars, pies, lines, and scattered dots. Your charts can be flat or 3-D. PowerPoint can create some complex charts, but keep your audience in mind. Ease of understanding should be your major goal. In this chapter, you'll learn how to:

- Use a datasheet to enter information for a graph
- Display datasheet information using different chart and graph formats
- Create a graphical representation of the hierarchy within a group

Organizing Data for the Chart

Before building a chart, organize the data you'll be depicting. Most charts compare two types of data, such as a budget where the amount spent on certain items is listed for a range of dates. PowerPoint provides a small example to get you started. Just replace the sample data with your own information.

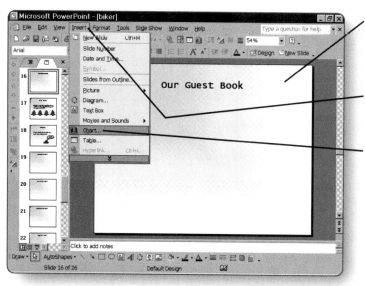

1. **Display** the **slide** on which you want to insert the chart. The slide will appear in Normal view.

2. **Click** on **Insert**. The Insert menu will appear.

3. **Click** on **Chart**. The sample chart and chart datasheet will appear on the slide.

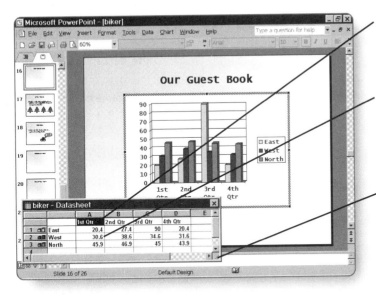

4. **Click** in a **cell** on the datasheet. The cell contents will be selected.

5. **Type** the **information** that you want to appear in the chart.

TIP

If your chart contains more data than the sample datasheet, resize the datasheet to display more rows and columns. To clear unused cell information, click on the cell and press the Delete key.

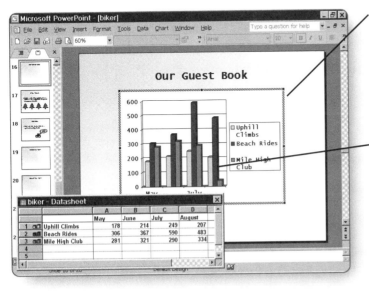

6. **Click** on a **blank area** of the slide. The datasheet will close and your information will display in the chart.

NOTE

If you need to make any changes to the information on the datasheet, double-click on the chart to open the datasheet.

Formatting the Chart

After you have entered all the data into the datasheet, it's time to create charts that will most effectively display the relationship between the two types of data you are comparing.

Selecting a Chart Type

The default chart type is the column chart. You'll also find an assortment of bar charts, pie charts, line charts, scatter charts, and much more. After you select a chart type, customize the chart to make it look the way you want.

1. **Double-click** on the **chart**. The datasheet will open and the menus will change so that only chart commands are listed.

2. **Click** on **Chart**. The Chart menu will appear.

3. **Click** on **Chart Type**. The Chart Type dialog box will open and the list of standard charts will display.

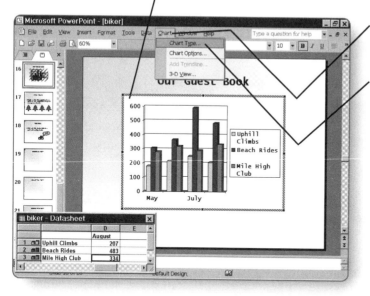

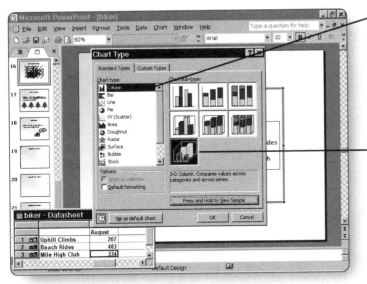

4. Click on the **category** of chart in the Chart type list. The category will be selected and the variations of the chart type will appear in the Chart sub-type area.

5. Click on a **style** of chart in the Chart sub-type area. The chart will be selected and you can read a description of the chart.

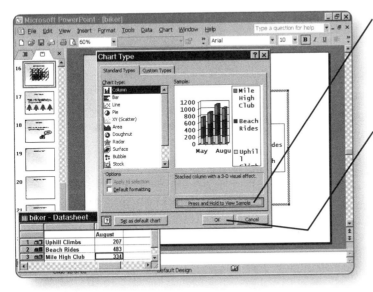

6. Click and **hold** the **Press and Hold to View Sample button** to see how the information in the datasheet will appear in the selected chart.

7. Click on **OK** when you have selected a chart type. The chart will be updated to display the selected chart type.

Naming the Chart

1. **Double-click** on the **chart**. The chart will be selected.

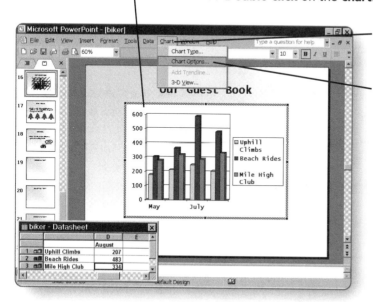

2. **Click** on **Chart**. The Chart menu will appear.

3. **Click** on **Chart Options**. The Chart Options dialog box will open and the Titles tab will be displayed. If the Titles tab is not selected, click on it.

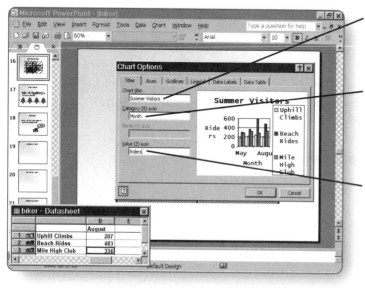

4. **Click** in the **Chart title text box** and **type** a **title** for the chart.

5. **Click** in the **Category (X) axis text box** and **type** a **label** for the information displayed on the X (horizontal) axis.

6. **Click** in the **Value (Z) axis text box** and **type** a **label** for the information displayed on the Z (vertical) axis.

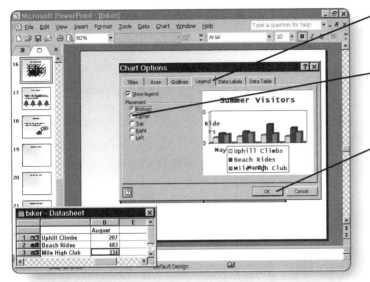

7. Click on the **Legend tab**. The legend options will appear.

8. Click on a **Placement option button** to move the legend to a different place on the slide.

9. Click on **OK**. Your changes will be applied to the chart.

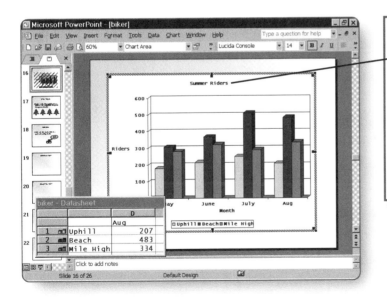

TIP

If you want to change the type style used for the chart text, right-click on a blank space next to the chart and select Format Chart Area. Change the type style from the Font tab.

Adding Color to the Chart

There are several different chart elements that you can format. The colors used in bar and pie charts can be changed. The border around the different chart elements can also be changed.

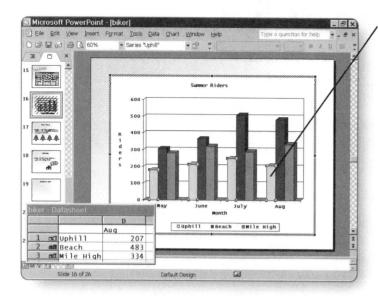

1. **Double-click** on the **chart element** that you want to change. A Format dialog box will open and the Patterns tab will be displayed.

2. Click on the **Custom option button** if you want to change the border that appears around the selected chart element. The option will be selected.

3. Click on the **list box arrow** for the Style, Color, and Weight of the line that is applied to the border. The selections will appear in the list boxes.

4. Click on a **color** in the Area section to change the color of the element. The color will be selected.

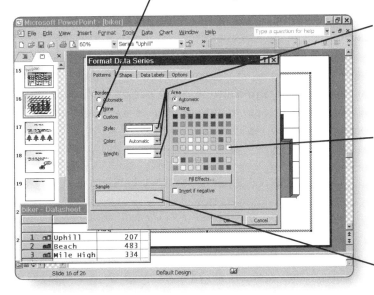

NOTE

The line and fill color you selected will display in the Sample area.

5. Click on the **Options tab**. The spacing options for chart elements will appear.

6. Click in the **Gap width text box** and **type** the **amount** of space that should appear between elements in a chart. This is useful for bar charts when you want more space between each bar.

7. Click on **OK**. Your changes will be applied to the chart.

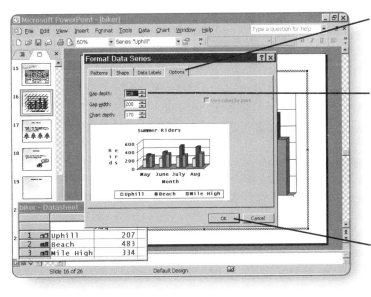

Creating an Organization Chart

For those times when you need to diagram the hierarchy of a group of people, add an organization chart to a slide. An organization chart shows the different reporting levels within a workgroup, or an entire company. You can show the people who are subordinate to a manager, the people who function as assistants and are not in the direct chain of command, and the interaction between co-workers.

Starting the Organization Chart

Before you start the organization chart, you'll need a list of people who will be represented in the chart, their job titles, or other information related to the group.

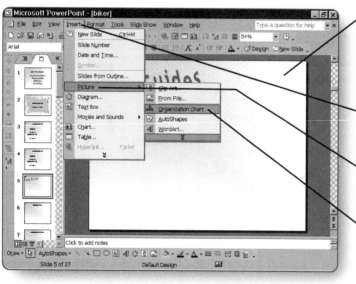

1. Open the **slide** that will contain the organization chart. The slide will appear in Normal view.

2. Click on **Insert**. The Insert menu will appear.

3. Click on **Picture**. A second menu will appear.

4. Click on **Organization Chart**. A sample organization chart will appear on the slide.

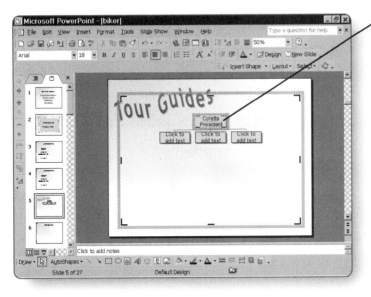

5. **Click** in a **box** on the organization chart. The box contents will be selected.

6. **Type** the **information** that you want to appear in the organization chart. Don't worry if the box is smaller than the text; the box will be resized to fit the text.

NOTE

To deselect the chart or chart elements, click on a blank area of the slide.

Adding Members to the Chart

The sample organization chart with which you started probably won't fit your needs. You'll want to add more boxes so that all the important people in your work group or organization are represented.

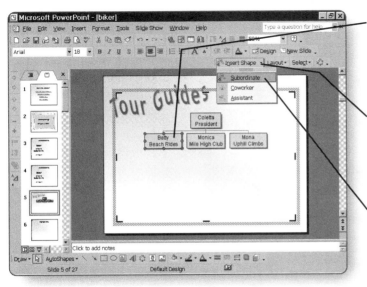

1. **Click** on the **box** in the organization chart to which you want to attach a new box. The box will be selected.

2. **Click** on the **Insert Shape down arrow button** on the Organization Chart toolbar. A menu will appear.

3. **Click** on the **type of box** to attach to the selected box.

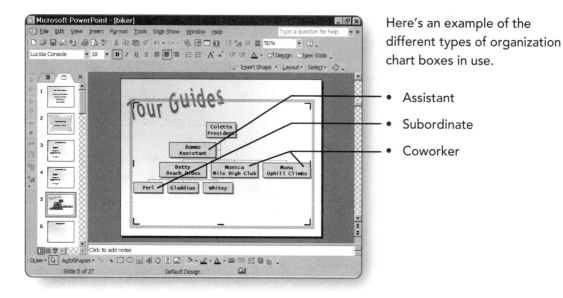

Here's an example of the different types of organization chart boxes in use.

- Assistant
- Subordinate
- Coworker

New boxes appear in horizontal rows in the organization chart. Here's how to change the alignment of boxes.

4. **Click** on the **box** to which the boxes that you want to align are attached. The box will be selected.

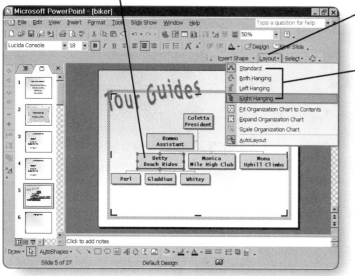

5. **Click** on the **Layout button**. A menu will appear.

6. **Click** on a **Hanging option**. The subordinate boxes will be rearranged.

Formatting the Organization Chart

The chart text can be formatted in a different font, and you can also format individual text elements. In addition, the different boxes can be changed to a different color and a different line style. Or, if you need some help, try out one of the styles from the Organization Chart Style Gallery.

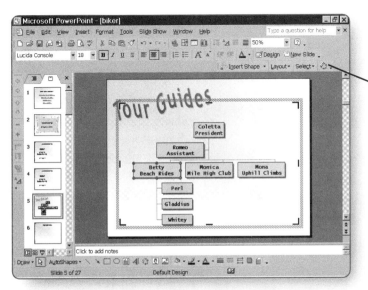

Selecting a Chart Style

1. **Click** on the **Autoformat button** on the Organization Chart toolbar. The Organization Chart Style Gallery will open.

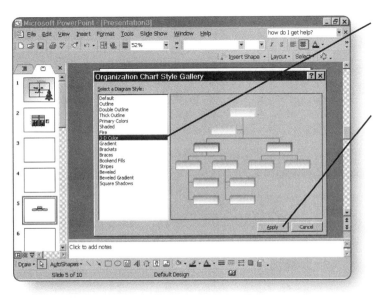

2. **Click** on a **chart style** in the Select a Diagram Style list. A sample of the chart style will appear in the preview area.

3. **Click** on **Apply**. The chart style will be applied to the organization chart.

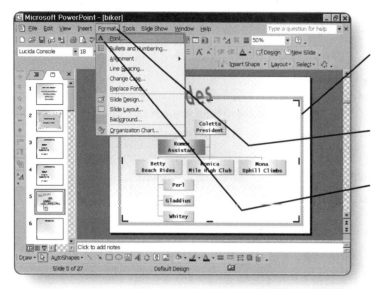

Formatting Text

1. Select the **organization chart**. An outline will appear around the chart.

2. Click on **Format**. The Format menu will appear.

3. Click on **Font**. The Font dialog box will open.

NOTE

Select the text and use the buttons on the Formatting toolbar to format individual text elements in the organization chart boxes.

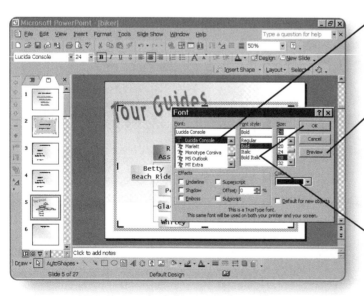

4. Click on an **option** in the Font, Font style, and Size list boxes. The font options will be selected.

5. Click on the **Preview button** to see how the font changes will look on the organization chart. The changes will appear on the slide in Normal view.

6. Click on **OK**. The selected text will be formatted.

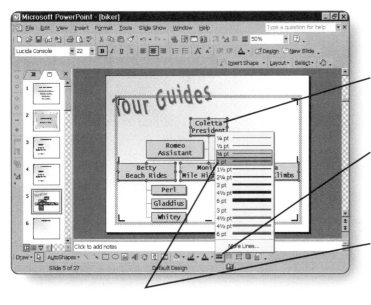

Changing the Line Style of a Box

1. Select the **box or boxes** that you want to change. The boxes will be selected.

2. Click on the **Line Style button** on the Drawing toolbar. A selection of line styles and weights will appear.

3. Click on a **line**. The line style will be applied to the selected boxes.

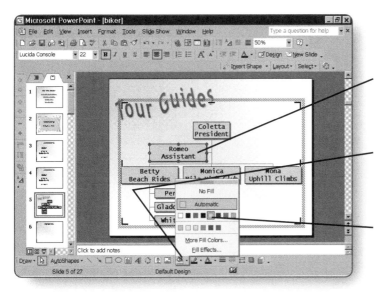

Changing the Color of a Box

1. Select the **box or boxes** that you want to change. The boxes will be selected.

2. Click on the **list box arrow** next to the Fill Color button. A selection of colors will appear.

3. Click on a **color**. The color will be applied to the selected boxes.

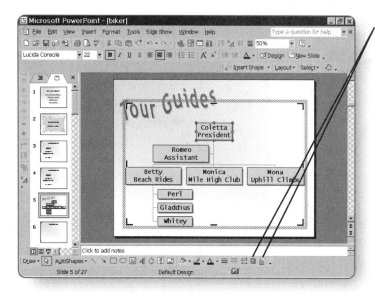

4. **Apply shadow** and **3-D effects** to organization chart boxes with the Shadow Style and 3-D Style buttons on the Drawing toolbar.

TIP

Chart elements can be animated. Right-click on a blank area of the chart and select Custom Animation. You'll learn about animations in Chapter 12, "Animating the Slide Show."

11

Diagramming Information

In Chapter 10, "Producing Charts and Graphs," you learned how to create organization charts and graphs based on spreadsheet data. These are not your only options when you need to diagram information. PowerPoint also contains diagram tools that make it easy to create other types of charts. In this chapter, you'll learn how to:

- Select a diagram type and add it to a PowerPoint slide
- Use text to emphasize diagram elements
- Add and rearrange shapes used in the diagram
- Give the diagram a stylish look

Inserting a Diagram

PowerPoint contains several types of diagrams and all can be customized to fit your needs. You can choose from circle diagrams (to show a continuous process), target diagrams (to show steps in a process to reach a desired result), radial diagrams (to illustrate the relationship between various elements), Venn diagrams (that show how elements overlap each other), and pyramid diagrams (to show the relationship between elements that rely on the same foundation). No matter which diagram you choose, all diagrams use the same tools to add additional elements and to customize the diagram shapes.

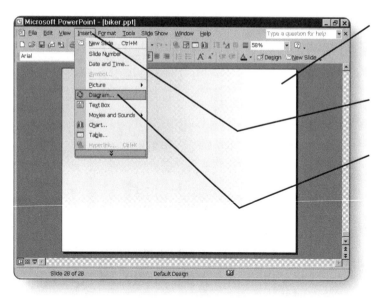

1. **Select** the **slide** on which you want to place the diagram. The slide will appear in Normal view.

2. **Click** on **Insert**. The Insert menu will appear.

3. **Click** on **Diagram**. The Diagram Gallery dialog box will open.

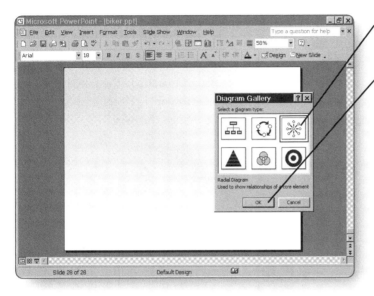

4. Click on a **diagram type**. The diagram will be selected.

5. Click on **OK**. The diagram will appear on the selected slide.

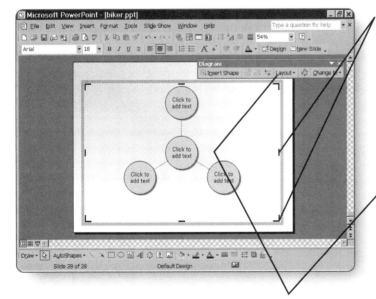

6. Click and **drag** the **resize handles** to fit the diagram on the slide. The outside border of the diagram will be resized and the diagram shapes will resize to fit within the border.

NOTE

If you want to increase the size of the diagram so that all shapes keep the same proportions, click on the Layout button on the Diagram toolbar and select Scale Diagram.

Using Text in a Diagram

Every shape on a diagram contains a text placeholder. In this placeholder, you can add text that describes the function of each element in the diagram. Once you've described each element, apply formatting to enhance the text.

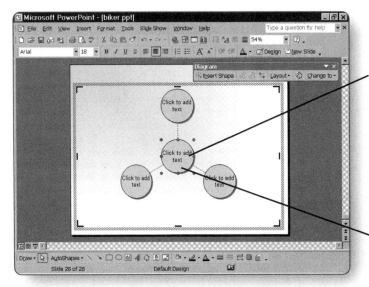

Adding Text to Shapes

1. Click on the text placeholder for the **shape** to which you want to add a text caption. The text placeholder will disappear and the cursor will appear in the middle of the shape.

NOTE

If you miss the text placeholder and select the shape instead, **click** on the **shape** a second time.

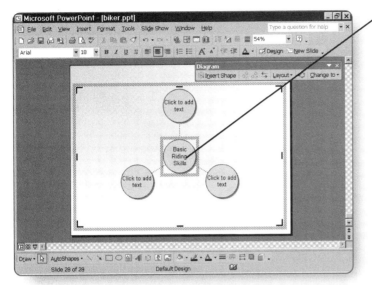

3. **Type** the **text**. To add multiple lines of text to a shape, press Enter at the end of each line. The text will appear inside the shape.

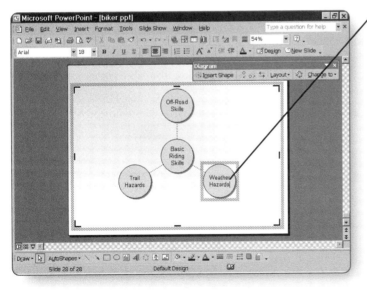

4. **Add text** to the other shapes in the diagram.

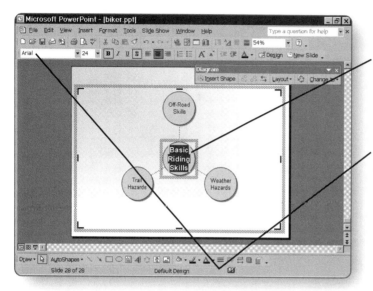

Formatting Text

1. Click and **drag** the **mouse pointer** over the text that you want to format. The text will be selected.

2. Format the **text**. Use any of the text formatting techniques that you learned about in Chapter 5, "Shaping Up Presentation Slides." You can change the font, font size, font color, paragraph alignment, and other font attributes from the Formatting toolbar.

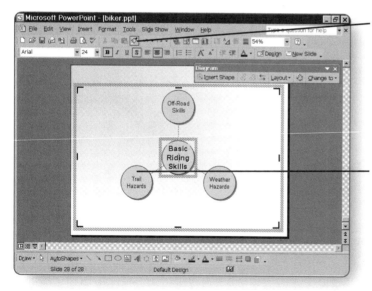

3. Double-click on the **Format Painter button** (the text in Step 1 should still be selected) to apply the same formatting to text in other shapes. The mouse pointer will change to a paintbrush.

4. Click and drag the mouse pointer over other text that you want to format. The formatting will be applied to the text in the selected shape.

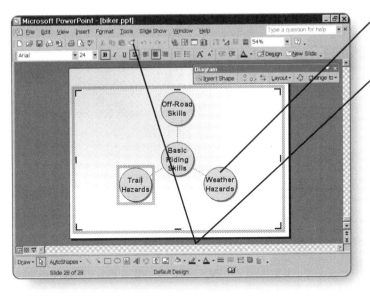

5. Apply the **formatting** to the other shapes in the diagram.

6. Click on the **Format Painter button** when you have finished.

Adding Shapes to the Diagram

Each diagram type contains a number of elements (or shapes) and you may find that there are too many or too few diagram elements. You can easily add more shapes to the diagram and rearrange the shapes to fit your needs.

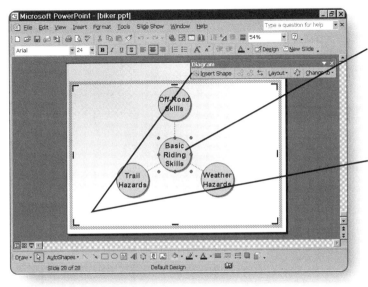

Inserting a Shape

1. Click on the shape border for the **diagram element** next to which you want to place the new shape. The shape will be selected.

2. Click on the **Insert Shape button** on the Diagram toolbar. A new shape will be added to the diagram.

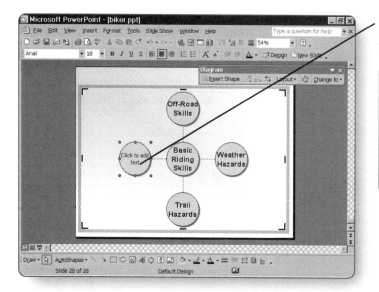

3. Add text to the shape and format the text as desired.

NOTE

To remove a shape, select the shape (by clicking on the shape border) and press the Delete key.

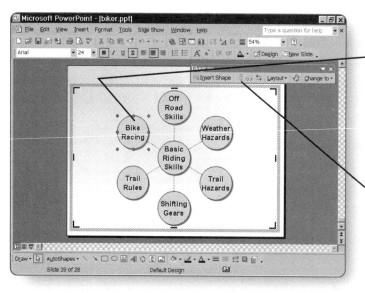

Moving the Shape

1. Click on the **shape border for the diagram element** that you want to move to a lower position in the diagram hierarchy. The shape will be selected.

2. Click on the **Move Shape Backward button**. The shape will be moved.

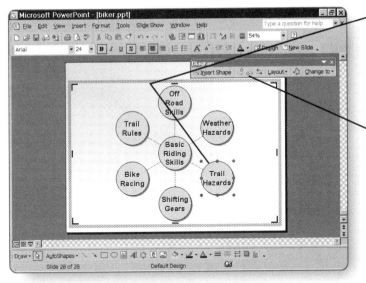

3. Click on the **shape border for the diagram element** that you want to move to a higher position in the diagram hierarchy.

4. Click on the **Move Shape Forward button**. The shape will be moved.

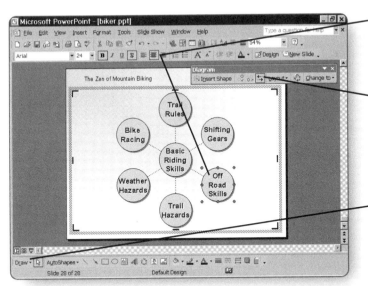

5. Click on the **shape** that you want to move to the top position in the diagram hierarchy.

6. Click on the **Reverse Diagram button**. The shape will be moved.

TIP

You can use a different shape for each element in the diagram. From the Drawing toolbar, click on the Draw button and move the mouse pointer to Change AutoShape. A list of the different types of shapes will appear and you can select a shape from any of the different shape types.

Applying Style to the Diagram

There are several ways in which you can give the diagram a different look. If you'd like a quick and easy way to stylize a diagram, use one of the AutoFormats. You can also apply a unique color and line style to each shape and add a background to the diagram area.

Using AutoFormats

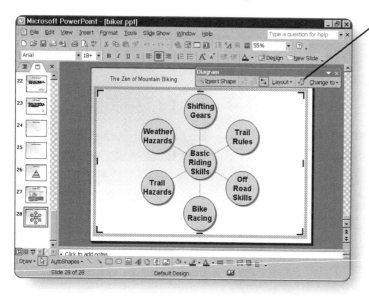

1. Click on the **AutoFormat button**. The Style Gallery dialog box for the diagram will open.

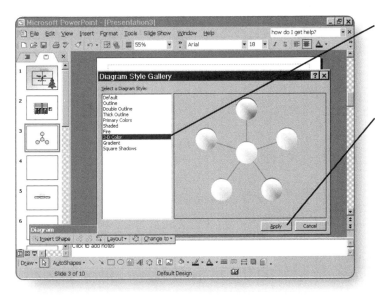

2. **Click** on a **style** from the Select a Diagram Style list. A preview of the selected style will appear in the Preview pane.

3. **Click** on **Apply** when you have made your selection. The diagram style will be updated.

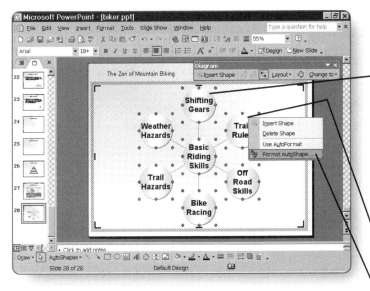

Adding Color to Diagram Shapes

1. **Click** on the **shape** to which you want to change the color or outline. If you want to select multiple shapes, press and hold the Shift key while you click on the other shapes that you want to format.

2. **Right-click** on the **shape**. A menu will appear.

3. **Click** on **Format AutoShape**. The Format AutoShape dialog box will open and the Colors and Lines tab will be displayed.

TIP

If the options in the Format AutoShape dialog box are grayed out, you will need to turn off the automatic formatting feature. Right-click on the shape and select Use AutoFormat. The check mark next to the command will disappear.

4. **Click** on the **Color list box arrow**. A selection of colors that you can apply to the shapes will appear.

5. **Click** on a **color**. You'll find more colors by clicking on More Colors. To add a gradient, texture, pattern, or picture to a shape, select Fill Effects. The color will be selected.

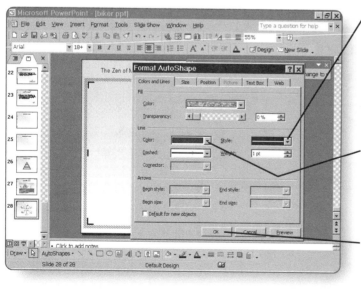

6. **Click** on the **Style list box arrow** and **select** a **line style** to apply to the outline of the shape. A selection of line widths that you can apply to the shape will appear.

7. **Click** the **Color list box arrow** and **select** a **color** for the line. The color will appear in the list box.

8. **Click** on **OK** when you are done. The shapes will be formatted with the new color and line style.

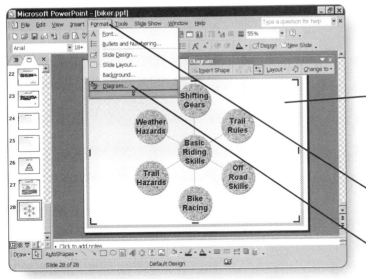

Changing the Diagram Background

1. **Select** the **diagram** to which you want to add a background color. The diagram will be selected.

2. **Click** on **Format**. The Format menu will appear.

3. **Click** on **Diagram**. The Format Diagram dialog box will appear.

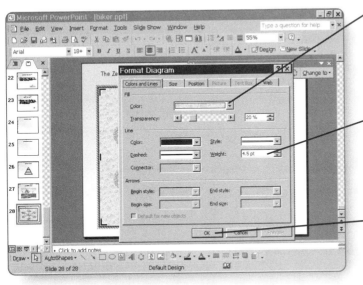

4. **Click** on a **color** in the Color list box. The color will be selected.

TIP

Place an outline around the diagram border to make the diagram stand out on the slide.

5. **Click** on **OK**. The color will be applied to the area inside the diagram border.

Part III Review Questions

1. If you don't have your own artwork to use in a presentation, where can you find a plethora of free clip art images? See "Working with Clip Art" in Chapter 7.

2. What is a fun and easy way to add an artistic flair to text? See "Designing with WordArt" in Chapter 7.

3. How do you use PowerPoint to control a scanner and automatically scan photographs onto presentation slides? See "Scanning Photographs" in Chapter 8.

4. Name some of the different ways in which PowerPoint can edit scanned images. See "Enhancing Digital Photographs" in Chapter 8.

5. Once you have created a table on a slide, how do you add new rows and columns? See "Modifying the Table" in Chapter 9.

6. Which different parts of a table can be decorated with colors and borders? See "Formatting the Table" in Chapter 9.

7. How do you create the datasheet needed to produce a chart or a graph? See "Organizing Data for the Chart" in Chapter 10.

8. What different types of charts can you create from the datasheet information? See "Formatting the Chart" in Chapter 10.

9. Name the different types of diagrams that are available in PowerPoint. See "Inserting a Diagram" in Chapter 11.

10. What is the easiest way to apply colorful effects to diagram shapes? See "Applying Style to the Diagram" in Chapter 11.

PART IV

Creating Special Effects

12

Animating the Slide Show

It's time to wake up your audience and roll a few objects across the screen during your slide show. How about a cool transition effect as each slide fades into the next slide? Or make bullet points fall from the sky as you introduce each point. The possibilities are endless. In this chapter, you'll learn how to:

- Use animation schemes to apply quick and easy slide transitions and animations
- Make slide elements march onto the slide in order
- Add cool effects so that one slide fades into the next slide

Rolling Objects Across the Screen

A new feature in PowerPoint is the collection of animated schemes that you can apply to the slides in a presentation. Animation schemes combine a slide transition and animated text objects.

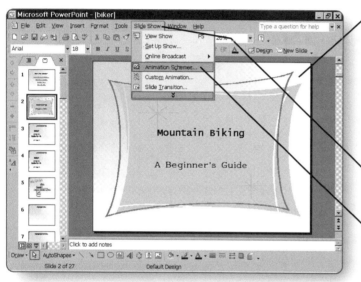

1. **Display** the **slide** to which you want to apply the animation. The slide will appear in Normal view. If you want to apply the animation to several slides, select the slides in Slide Sorter view.

2. **Click** on **Slide Show**. The Slide Show menu will appear.

3. **Click** on **Animation Schemes**. The Slide Design task pane will appear and the available slide animations will be listed.

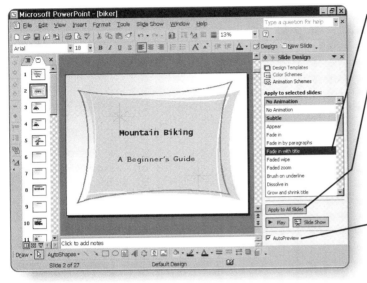

4. **Click** on an **animation scheme**. The animation will be applied to the selected slides.

5. **Click** on the **Apply to All Slides button** if you want every slide in the presentation to use the same animation scheme.

NOTE

Place a check mark in the AutoPreview check box if you want to watch the animation in action when one animation scheme is selected.

Animating Text

When outstanding 3-D text and images are too static for your tastes, try your hand at animation. You can apply a number of customizable animation effects so that objects fly, slide, flip, and dissolve right before your eyes. You can also organize a series of objects so that they perform object by object.

TIP

If you used one of the animation schemes, follow these directions to customize the animation effect and speed of the different screen elements.

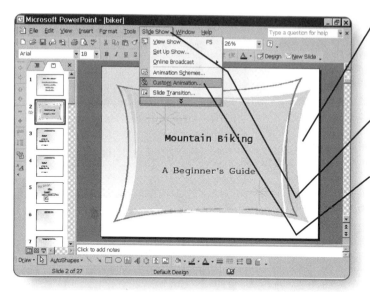

1. **Open** the **slide** that contains the element that you want to animate. The slide will appear in Normal view.

2. **Click** on **Slide Show**. The Slide Show menu will appear.

3. **Click** on **Custom Animation**. The Custom Animation task pane will appear.

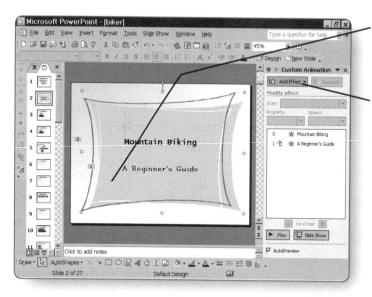

4. **Click** on the **element** on the slide that you want to animate. The element will be selected.

5. **Click** on the **Add Effect button** on the task pane. A menu will appear.

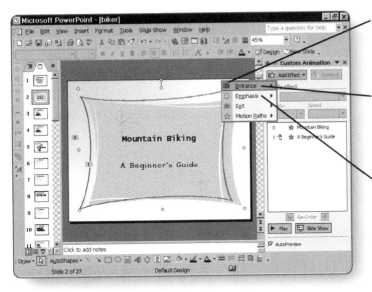

6. Click on a **category** of effects. A second menu will appear.

- When you want slide elements to enter the slide when it displays, look through the list of Entrance effects.

- Effects that occur while the slide is displayed are found on the Emphasis menu.

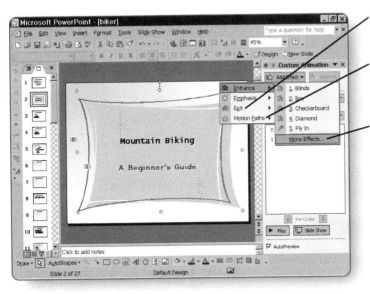

- To make an element leave the slide, choose an Exit effect.

- Elements can follow a custom path across the slide using Motion Paths.

7. Click on **More Effects.** Or if you are using a motion path, **click** on **More Motion Paths.** A separate window with a list of special effects will appear.

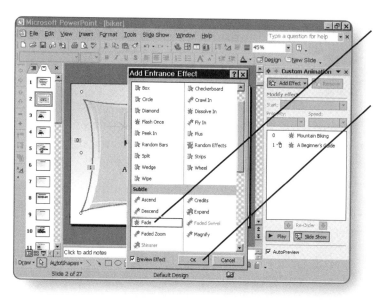

8. Click on an **effect**. A preview of the effect will play in the Normal view.

9. Click on **OK** when you have selected an animation effect. The animation will be applied to the slide elements. You can now modify the animation.

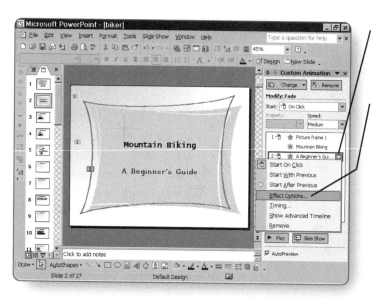

10. Click the **down arrow** next to an animation object. A menu will appear.

11. Click on **Effect Options**. The options for the selected animation will appear. The Effect tab should be selected.

NOTE

The effect options for each animation are different. Experiment with effects. See if you can imitate some of the effects you've seen in other presentations.

12. Click the **Sound list box arrow** and select a sound to play during the animation. The selected sound will appear in the list box.

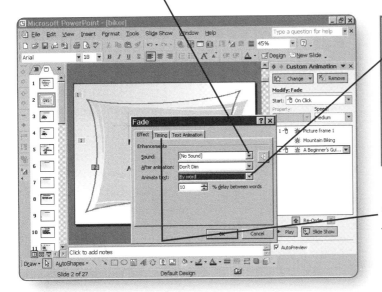

NOTE

If you are animating a text element, you use the Animate text option to animate the text as a single unit, word by word, or letter by letter.

13. Click on the **Timing tab**. The timing options will appear.

14. **Click** the **Start list box arrow** and **select** when the animation will start. The selected option will appear in the list box.

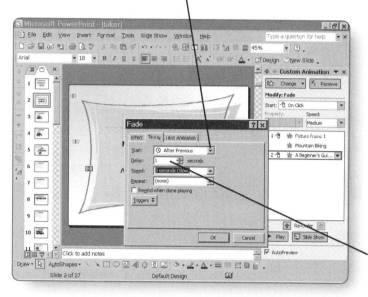

- On Click starts an animation with a mouse click on the slide.

- With Previous starts the animation at the same time as the previous item in the animation list.

- After Previous starts the animation when the previous item in the animation list finishes.

15. **Type** the **number** of seconds in the Delay text box.

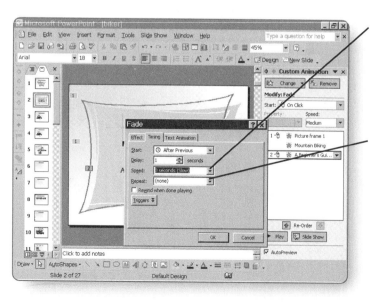

16. **Click** the **Speed list box arrow** and **select** the **speed** at which you want the animation to play. The speed will appear in the list box.

17. **Click** the **Repeat list box arrow** and **select** the **number** of times to repeat the animation on the slide. The selected number will appear in the list box.

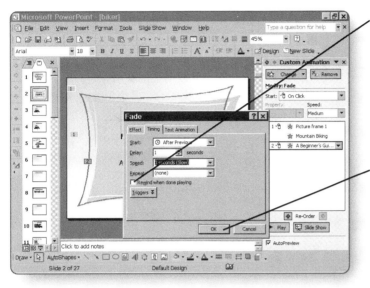

18. Place a **check mark** in the Rewind when done playing check box if you want objects to be in the same position as they were when the animation started. A check mark will appear in the check box.

19. Click on **OK** when you are finished customizing the animation. The dialog box will close.

Using Slide Transitions

You just saw how to apply animation to individual objects on a slide. You can also apply animation to a slide. This type of animation is a transition effect that appears when a slide displays during a slide show. Transition effects cause an entire slide to dissolve, fade, or break up into pieces when moving from one slide to the next.

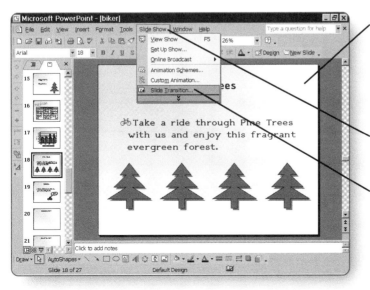

1. Open the **slide** to which you want to apply the transition. The slide will appear in Normal view. Or, select several slides from the Slide Sorter view.

2. Click on **Slide Show**. The Slide Show menu will appear.

3. Click on **Slide Transition**. The Slide Transition task pane will appear.

4. **Click** on a **slide transition**. The transition will be selected and a preview of the transition will appear if the AutoPreview check box is selected.

5. **Click** the **Speed list box arrow** and **select** the speed at which you want the transition to play. The speed will appear in the list box.

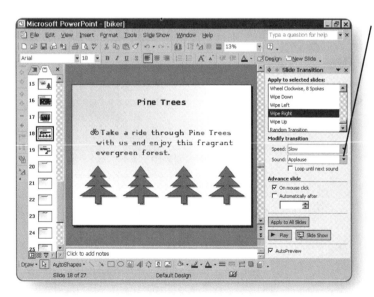

6. **Click** the **Sound list box arrow** and **select** a sound to play during a slide transition. The sound will appear in the list box.

TIP

If you want to play a sound that you have stored on your computer, select the Other Sound option located at the bottom of the list.

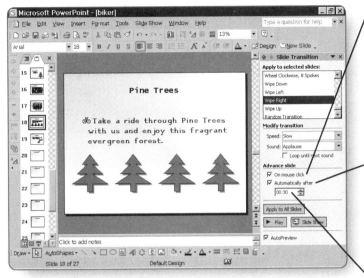

7. **Place** a **check mark** in the On mouse click check box if you want to advanced from the selected slide to the next slide by clicking on a slide during a slide show. A check mark will appear in the check box.

8. **Place** a **check mark** in the Automatically after check box if you want the slide to advance automatically after a set number of seconds.

9. **Type** the **number of seconds** the slide should display onscreen before automatically advancing to the next screen.

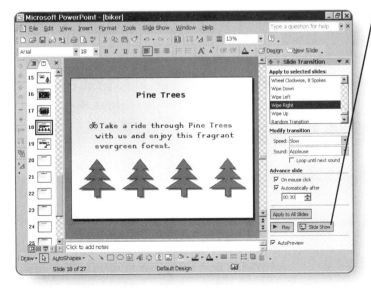

10. **Click** on the **Slide Show button** to start the slide show and watch your animation in action. Use the left and right arrow keys to advanced from slide to slide, if automatic timing has not been applied.

Customizing Animations

You may find that you need to make some changes to the animations you applied to slides and slide elements.

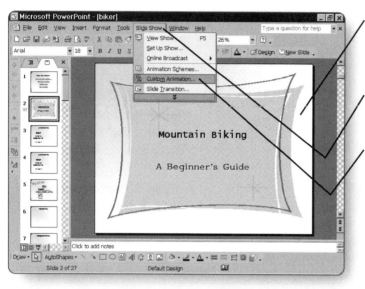

1. **Open** the **slide** that contains the animation that you want to change.

2. **Click** on **Slide Show**. The Slide Show menu will appear.

3. **Click** on **Custom Animation**. The Custom Animation task pane will appear.

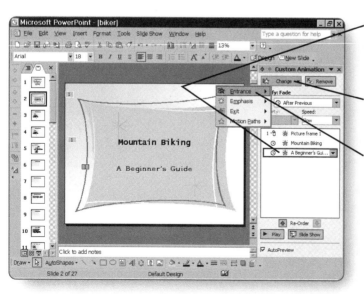

4. **Click** on the **animation** that you want to change. The animation will be selected.

5. **Click** on the **Change button**. The list of effects will appear.

6. **Click** on an **effect**. The new effect will be applied to the slide element.

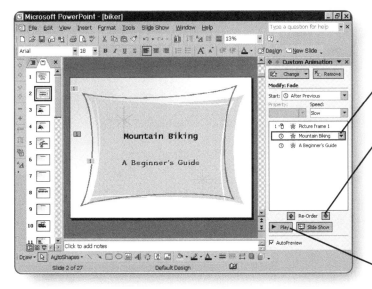

You can change the order in which an animation appears on the slide.

7. **Click** on the **animation**. The animation will be selected.

8. **Click** on the **up or down Re-Order button**. The selected animation will move positions in the list.

NOTE

Click on the Play button to see your animations in action.

13

Moving Along with Multimedia

Another way to make a slide show interesting and keep your audience's attention is to add music and video to the slide show. You may have music that you've created using your computer's MIDI equipment and software, or you may have a music CD that you'd like to play. Also, if you have digital video files, you can easily show videos during a slide show. In this chapter, you'll learn how to:

- Play a sound file as background music for a single slide
- Listen to a CD while playing a slide show
- Watch movies during a slide show presentation

Playing Background Music

PowerPoint gives you the ability to play a background sound while a slide is displayed during a slide show. If a presentation does not use a live presenter, you may want to add some background music that viewers can listen to while they watch the slide show. If you do use a presenter to control the slide show, you may still want to add background music to give the presenter a little help.

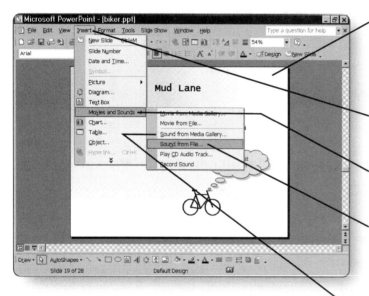

1. **Display** the **slide** that will play music when displayed during the slide show. The slide will appear in Normal view.

2. **Click** on **Insert**. The Insert menu will appear.

3. **Click** on **Movies and Sounds**. A second menu will appear.

4. **Click** on **Sound from File**. The Insert Sound dialog box will open.

NOTE

You'll also find music files in the Media Gallery. Just click on the Sound from Media Gallery menu item.

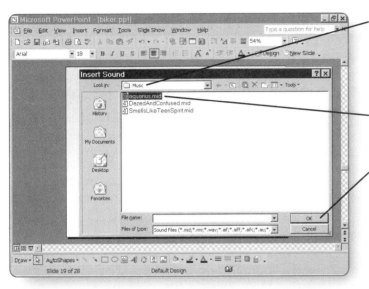

5. Navigate to the **folder** that contains the sound file. The folder name will appear in the Look in list box.

6. Click on the **sound file**. The file will be selected.

7. Click on **OK**. A confirmation dialog box will appear.

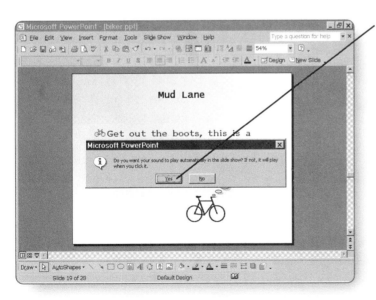

8. Click on **Yes** if you want the sound to play when the slide appears during the slide show. The sound icon appears on the slide.

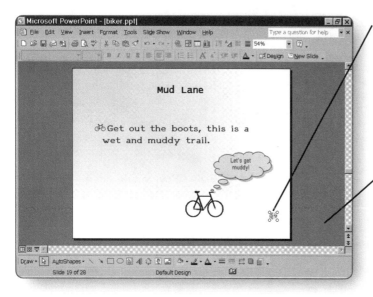

9. Click and **drag** the **sound icon** to a different location on the slide. The sound icon can be moved to any location on the slide.

TIP

If you don't want to see the sound icon on the slide, drag it off the slide.

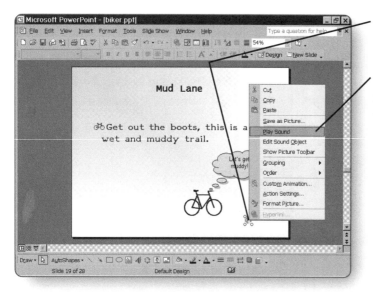

10. Right-click on the **sound icon**. A menu will appear.

11. Click on **Play Sound**. You should hear the music play on the computer sound system.

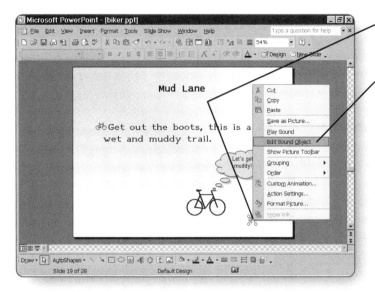

12. **Right-click** on the **sound icon** again. A menu will appear.

13. **Click** on **Edit Sound Object**. The Sound Options dialog box will open.

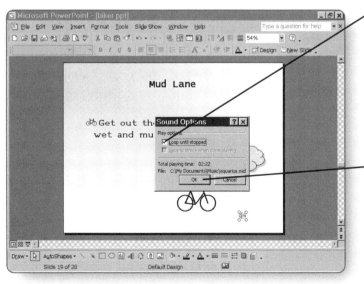

14. **Click** in the **Loop until stopped** check box if you want the music file to play continuously while the slide is displayed during the slide show. A check mark will appear in the check box.

15. **Click** on **OK**. The settings will be applied to the sound file.

Playing Audio CDs

Another way to play music while a slide is displayed during the slide show is to pop a music CD into the computer and let PowerPoint play the CD tracks that you specify.

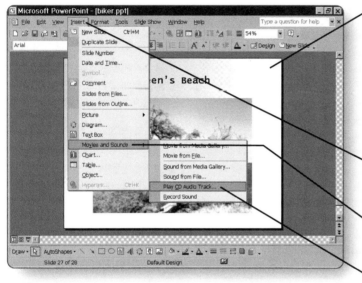

1. **Display** the **slide** for which you want to play the CD track. The slide will appear in Normal view.

2. **Place** the **CD** that you want to play in the CD-ROM drive.

3. **Click** on **Insert**. The Insert menu will appear.

4. **Click** on **Movies and Sounds**. A second menu will appear.

5. **Click** on **Play CD Audio Track**. The Movie and Sound Options dialog box will open.

6. **Click** in the **Loop until stopped check box** if you want the CD track to play continuously. A check mark will appear in the check box.

7. **Click** in the **Start Track text box** and **type** the **track number** for the first track on the CD that you want to play.

8. **Click** in the **End Track text box** and **type** the **track number** for the last track on the CD that you want to play.

9. **Click** on **OK**. A confirmation dialog box will appear.

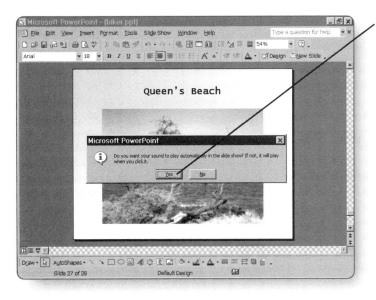

10. **Click** on **Yes**. The CD icon will appear on the slide and the CD will play automatically when the slide appears during the slide show.

11. Click and **drag** the **CD icon**. The CD icon will be moved to a different location on the slide.

NOTE

When you deliver the presentation, the music CD will need to be in the computer's CD-ROM drive in order to play the music.

Going to the Movies

Digitized video files can also be used on PowerPoint slides to play a video during the slide show. For instance, you may have a product demonstration video that may be interesting to your slide show audience. Instead of playing the video on a separate display, just insert the video onto the slide.

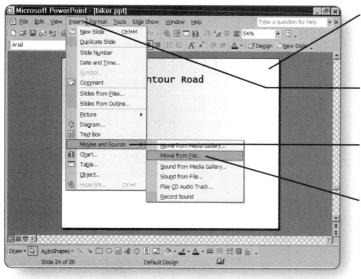

1. Open the **slide** in which the video will appear. The slide will appear in Normal view.

2. Click on **Insert**. The Insert menu will appear.

3. Click on **Movies and Sounds**. A second menu will appear.

4. Click on **Movie From File**. The Insert Movie dialog box will open.

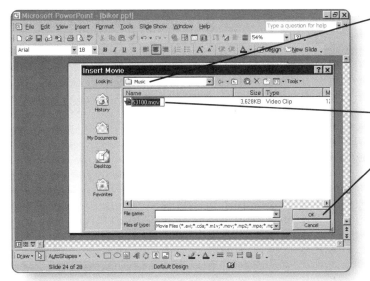

5. Navigate to the **folder** that contains the movie file. The folder name will appear in the Look in list box.

6. Click on the **movie file**. The file will be selected.

7. Click on **OK**. A confirmation dialog box will appear.

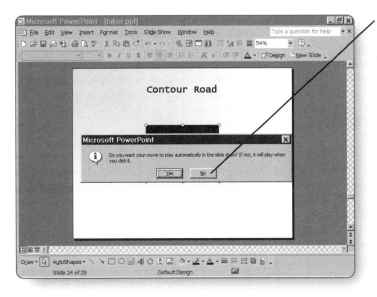

8. Click on **No** if you want the movie to start when you click on the movie icon. The movie appears on the slide.

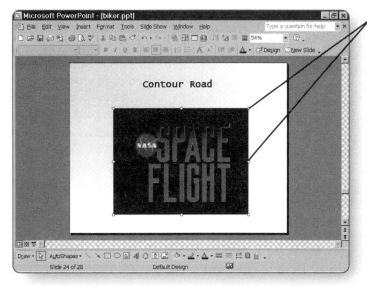

9. **Click** and **drag** the **resize handles**. The movie will be resized. You may want to resize the movie so that it takes up the entire slide area.

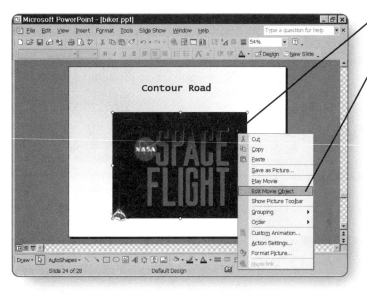

10. **Right-click** on the **movie**. A menu will appear.

11. **Click on Edit Movie Object**. The Movie Options dialog box will open.

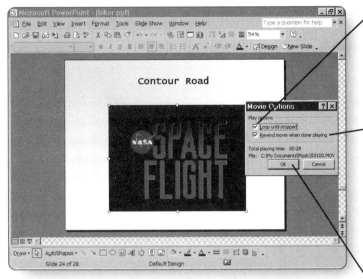

12. **Click** in the **Loop until stopped check box** if you want the move to play continuously. A check mark will appear in the check box.

13. **Click** in the **Rewind movie when done playing check box** if you want the movie to automatically rewind to the beginning when the movie has finished playing. A check mark will appear in the check box.

14. **Click** on **OK**. The settings will be applied to the movie.

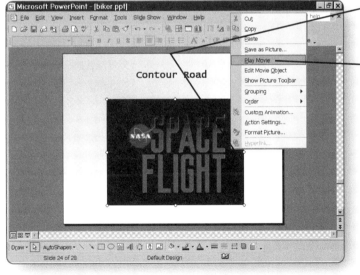

15. **Right-click** on the **movie** again. A menu will appear.

16. **Click** on **Play Movie**. The movie will begin to play on the slide so that you can test out the display.

Watching Windows Media Files

Another way to watch a video or listen to music during a slide show is to use the Windows Media Player to control the movie or sound file. With the Windows Media Player, you can use the player controls to start and stop the movie or the music.

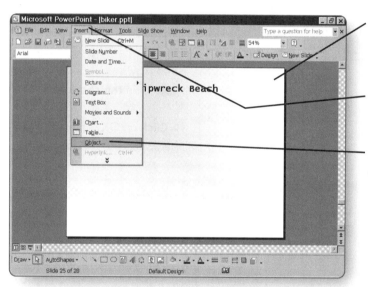

1. **Open** the **slide** in which the media file will be played. The slide will appear in Normal view.

2. **Click** on **Insert**. The Insert menu will appear.

3. **Click** on **Object**. The Insert Object dialog box will open.

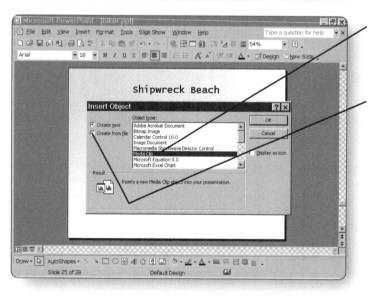

4. **Click** on **Media Clip** in the Object type list box. The option will be selected.

5. **Click** on the **Create from file option button**. The option will be selected and the dialog box will change.

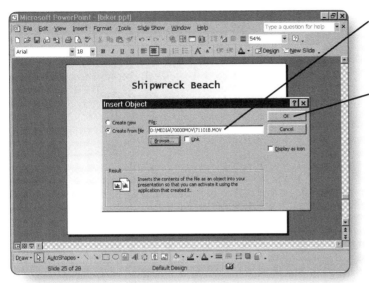

6. Type the **path and name** for the media file in the File text box.

7. Click on **OK**. The movie or music icon will appear on the slide.

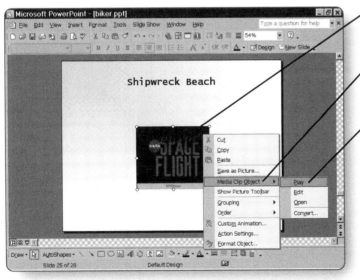

8. Right-click on the **movie or music icon**. A menu will appear.

9. Click on **Media Clip Object**. A second menu will appear.

10. Click on **Play**. The movie will play in the Windows Media Player.

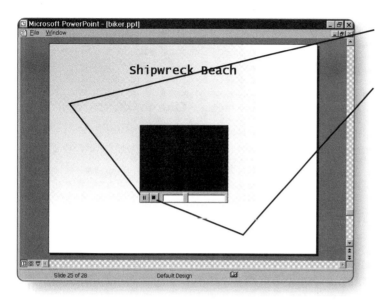

11. **Click** on the **Pause button** to temporarily stop the movie.

12. **Click** on the **Stop button** to stop the movie.

Part IV Review Questions

1. Where can you find animation schemes that include slide transitions and animated text? See "Rolling Objects Across the Screen" in Chapter 12.

2. What are some of the different ways in which text can move on a slide? See "Animating Text" in Chapter 12.

3. How do you change the speed at which text moves across a slide during a slide show? See "Animating Text" in Chapter 12.

4. How do you apply a transition between one slide and another during a slide show? See "Using Slide Transitions" in Chapter 12.

5. Is it possible to play a sound file when you move from one slide to another during a slide show? See "Using Slide Transitions" in Chapter 12.

6. Can a single music file be played during an entire slide show presentation? See "Playing Background Music" in Chapter 13.

7. How do you add sounds to a slide? See "Playing Background Music" in Chapter 13.

8. Does the music that you want to play during a slide show need to be digitized into one of the sound file formats? See "Playing Audio CDs" in Chapter 13.

9. Explain how to set up a video file so that it plays automatically when the slide on which it resides appears during the slide show. See "Going to the Movies" in Chapter 13.

10. How do you set up a video file so that you have controls to start and stop the movie? See "Watching Windows Media Files" in Chapter 13.

PART V

Getting Ready for the Show

14

Working with Other Office Applications

Taking items that you've created in one program (such as text or graphic images) and using them in another program became a reality with the invention of OLE (Object Linking and Embedding). This may sound like a complex concept, but it simply allows you to copy an item, for example a spreadsheet created in Excel, and place it on a PowerPoint slide. The easy part is that you don't need to know anything about converting file formats. You have several options from which to choose when sharing information between Office applications. In this chapter, you'll learn how to:

- Copy items using the Office Clipboard
- Change text formatting when copying an item
- Drag and drop items between Office applications
- Link and embed items

Using the Office Clipboard

The Office Clipboard is an enhanced version of the Windows Clipboard. Instead of being able to store only one item at a time, the Office Clipboard can store up to 24 items that you can copy among all Office programs (not just within PowerPoint).

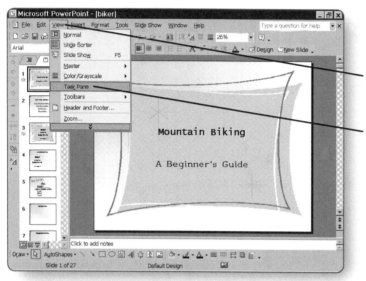

Displaying the Clipboard

1. **Click** on **View**. The View menu will appear.

2. **Click** on **Task Pane**. The Task Pane will appear.

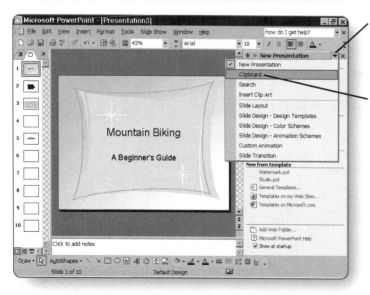

3. **Click** on the **Task Pane down arrow**. A list of available task panes will appear.

4. **Click** on **Clipboard**. The Clipboard task pane will appear.

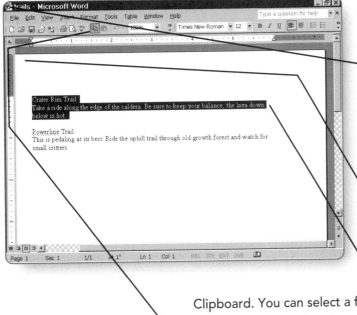

Adding Items to the Clipboard

1. **Open** the **Office application** in which you created the document that contains information that you want to copy. The Office application will appear on the screen.

2. **Open** the **document file**. The file will appear in the application window.

3. **Select** the **information** that you want to add to the Clipboard. You can select a few words, a paragraph, a bullet list, a picture, or a drawing object.

4. **Click** on the **Copy button** on the Standard toolbar. The item will be copied to the Office Clipboard.

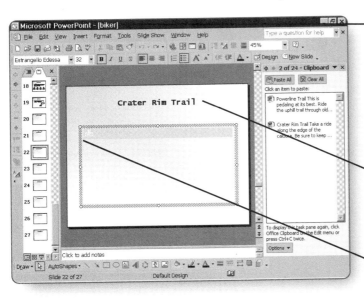

5. **Display** the **PowerPoint presentation file** into which you want to paste the information you copied in Step 4. PowerPoint will appear on the screen and you'll see the item added to the Clipboard.

6. **Display** the **slide** that will contain the copied information. The slide will appear in Normal view.

7. **Click** in the **place** where you want to insert an item from the Clipboard. The insertion bar will appear on the slide.

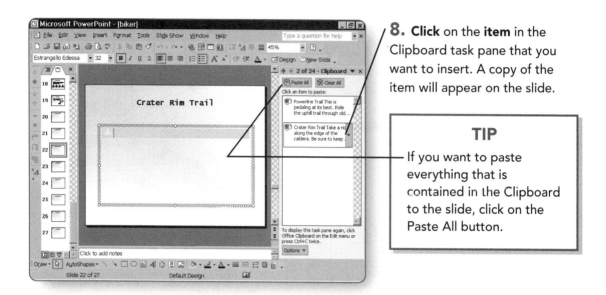

8. **Click** on the **item** in the Clipboard task pane that you want to insert. A copy of the item will appear on the slide.

TIP

If you want to paste everything that is contained in the Clipboard to the slide, click on the Paste All button.

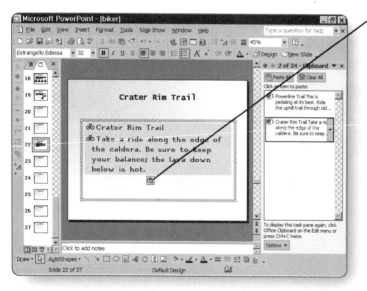

Inserted text takes on the formatting of the slide and a Paste Options button appears next to the text. If you want to use the original formatting, you can return the text to the original formatting with this button.

NOTE

After you have copied an item from the Clipboard onto a slide, you can change the size, reformat the text, or make any other changes you might want.

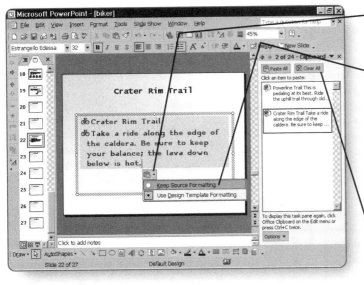

9. Click on the **Paste Options button**. A menu will appear.

10. Click on **Keep Source Formatting** if you want to retain the original formatting of the text. The text format will change back to the way it appeared in the Office application from which it was copied.

11. Click on the **Clear All button** on the Clipboard task pane. The contents of the Clipboard will be emptied.

Formatting Data When Pasting

There may be times when you want to copy information, but the way the text is formatted will not work in the document you are creating. For example, you may want to copy some text you created in a Web page, but you don't want the HTML formatting in your presentation. You can use a special command to make this task easy.

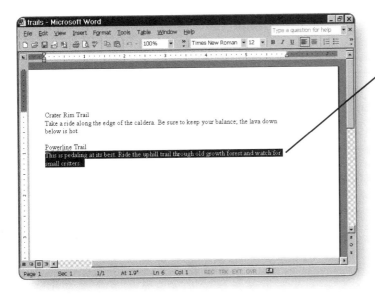

1. Select the **text** that you want to copy. The text will be highlighted.

2. Press Ctrl+C. The selected text will be copied to the Clipboard.

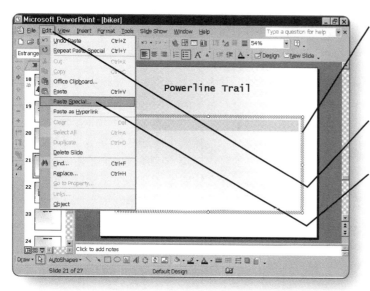

3. Click in the **place** where you want to insert the copied text. The insertion bar will appear in the selected place.

4. Click on **Edit**. The Edit menu will appear.

5. Click on **Paste Special**. The Paste Special dialog box will open.

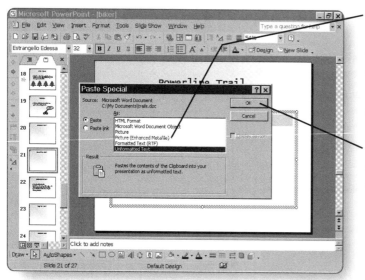

6. Click on the **formatting option** in the As list box that you want to apply to the copied item when it is pasted into the new place. The option will be selected.

7. Click on **OK**. The pasted text will appear in the selected format.

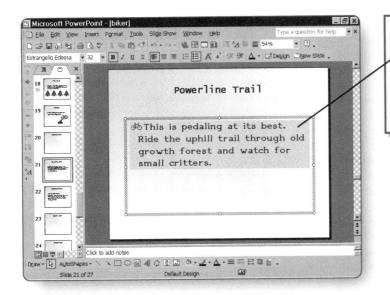

NOTE

Unformatted text will take on the formatting of the paragraph into which it is inserted.

Dragging and Dropping between Applications

The fastest way to move items between two programs is to use the drag-and-drop method. When you use this method, the copied text will take on the default formatting of the slide into which it is pasted.

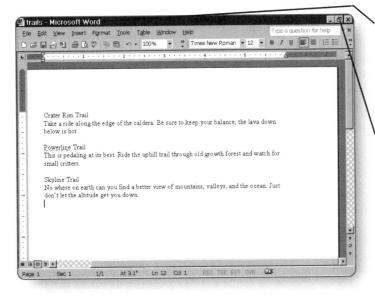

1. Open the **file** containing the information that you want to copy to a PowerPoint slide. Scroll to display the information in the program window.

2. Click on the **Restore button** located at the top right of the program window. The program window will decrease so that you can see the desktop.

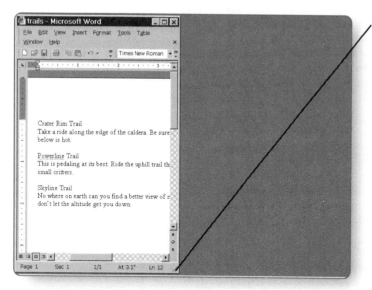

3. **Resize** the **program window** so that it takes up only half of the desktop. Click and drag the corner of the window to the desired location.

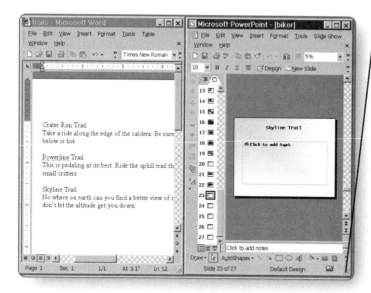

4. **Restore** and **resize** the **PowerPoint program window** so that it takes up the other half of the desktop.

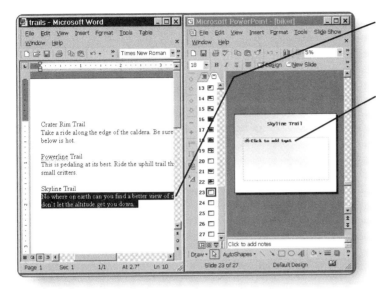

5. **Select** the **items** that you want to copy. The items will be highlighted.

6. **Press** and **hold** the **right mouse button** on the selected items and drag to the location in the PowerPoint file where you want to copy the items. The mouse pointer will have a box attached to it.

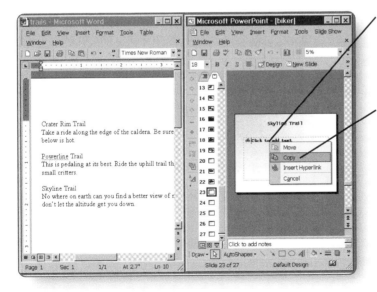

7. **Release** the **mouse button** at the desired location in PowerPoint. A shortcut menu will appear.

8. **Click** on **Copy**. The items will be copied to the new location within PowerPoint.

Linking and Embedding Documents

Linking and embedding are methods of copying objects (such as files or images) into another file so that the linked or embedded objects can be edited from the program in which they were created (not the program into which they were copied). When a linked file is modified in the program in which it was created, the changes to the file will be seen in PowerPoint. When an embedded file is modified in the program in which it was created, the information in PowerPoint does not change.

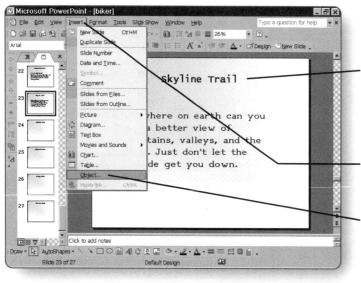

Linking a File to a PowerPoint Slide

1. **Open** the **slide** in which you want to create a link to an object. The slide will appear in the Normal view.

2. **Click** on **Insert**. The Insert menu will appear.

3. **Click** on **Object**. The Insert Object dialog box will open.

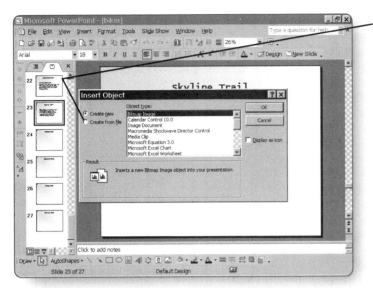

4. **Click** on the **Create from file option button**. The option will be selected, and the Insert Object dialog box will change.

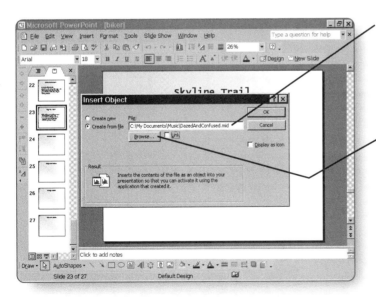

5. **Click** in the **File text box** and **type** the **name** of the file that you want to link to the slide.

NOTE

If you don't know the path and filename, click the Browse button and search for the file.

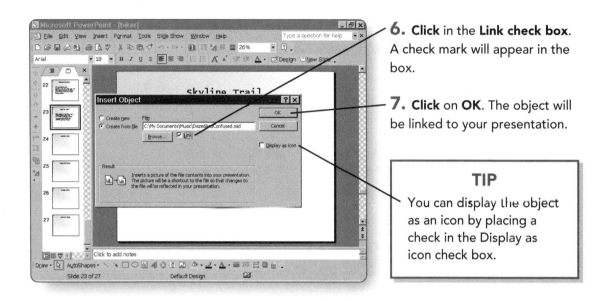

6. **Click** in the **Link check box**. A check mark will appear in the box.

7. **Click** on **OK**. The object will be linked to your presentation.

TIP

You can display the object as an icon by placing a check in the Display as icon check box.

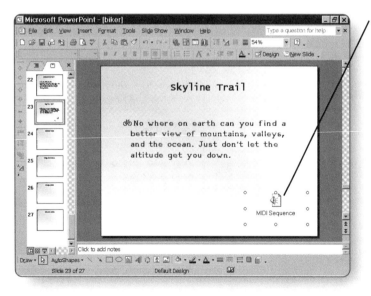

The object will appear on the slide. You can resize the object if needed.

Embedding Documents

To embed an object into a PowerPoint slide, you'll follow almost the same steps as you did to link the object. The only difference is that you can ignore the Link check box in the Insert Object dialog box.

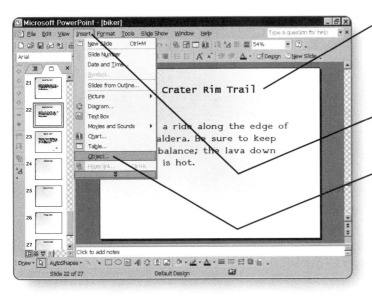

1. **Open** the **slide** in which you want to embed an object. The slide will appear in the Normal view.

2. **Click** on **Insert**. The Insert menu will appear.

3. **Click** on **Object**. The Insert Object dialog box will open.

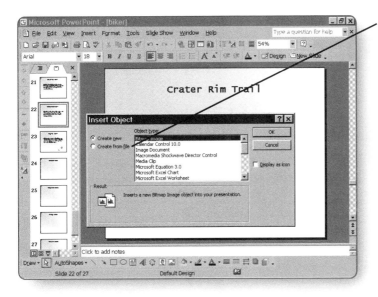

4. **Click** on the **Create from file option button**. The option will be selected and the Insert Object dialog box will change.

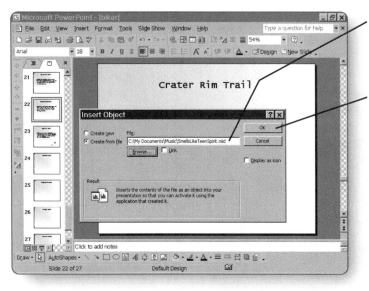

5. Click in the **File text box** and type the **name** of the file that you want to link to the slide.

6. Click on **OK**. The object will be embedded in your presentation.

Creating a New Embedded Object

You can embed an object that you haven't created yet. You can create this object in PowerPoint by using the toolbars and menus found in the program that is the default program for the file type of the object.

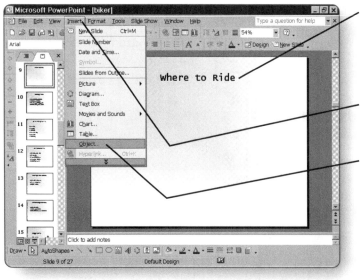

1. Open the **slide** in which you want to create an embedded object. The slide will appear in the Normal view.

2. Click on **Insert**. The Insert menu will appear.

3. Click on **Object**. The Insert Object dialog box will open.

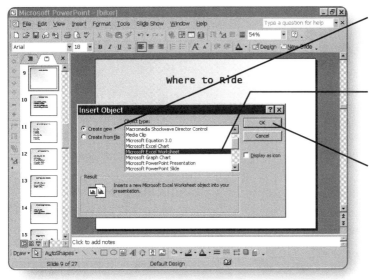

4. **Click** on the **Create new option button**. The option will be selected.

5. **Click** on the **type of object** you want to create. The object type will be selected.

6. **Click** on **OK**. The application that will create the type of file you selected will open in a small window within the PowerPoint slide.

7. **Create** the **object**. The new object will be displayed in the other program window.

8. **Click** outside the **PowerPoint slide**. The object will be added to the slide.

NOTE

If a separate application opened, click on the Close button for that application after you create the desired object. The program will close, and the object you just created will appear on the PowerPoint slide.

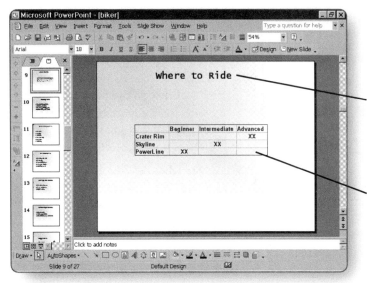

Modifying a Linked or Embedded Object

1. **Open** the **slide** that contains the linked or embedded object you want to modify. The slide will appear in the Normal view.

2. **Double-click** on the **object**. The object will appear in the program in which it was created. For some Office programs, a small window in which you can make your changes will appear on the slide.

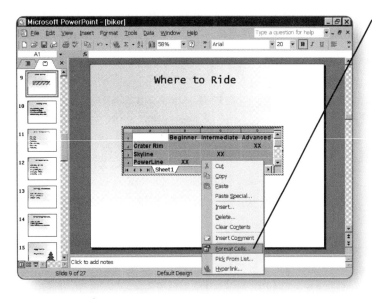

3. **Make changes** as needed.

4. **Click** on the **Close button** to close the program that opened to allow you to modify the object. The program will close and the object on the slide will be changed.

NOTE

If a window opened on the slide in which you made the changes, click outside the window to close it.

15

Collaborating with PowerPoint

So far, you've been working on a presentation by yourself. It's easy to control a project if you're the only person you have to manage. But, what do you do when several people are involved? You need a method for managers and reviewers to share their input. One way to route a presentation is through e-mail. Once reviewers have their copy of the presentation, they can place comments on slides. In this chapter, you'll learn how to:

- E-mail a presentation to other people for review
- Place comments on a presentation slide
- Incorporate comments made by reviewers

Routing the Presentation to Reviewers

Every work group has its own method for dealing with document reviews and edits, but they each follow the same basic process. First, files are set up for review and then distributed to each reviewer. Many times, the distribution is done with e-mail.

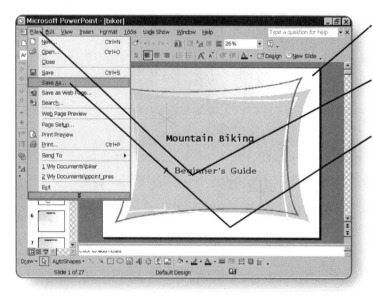

1. Open the **presentation** that you want to send out for review.

2. Click on **File**. The File menu will appear.

3. Click on **Save As**. The Save As dialog box will open.

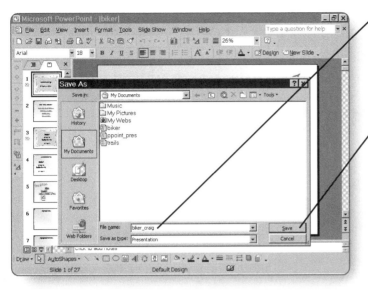

4. **Type** a new **file name** for the presentation in the File name text box. The file name should include the name of the reviewer to which the file will be e-mailed.

5. **Click** on **Save**. A copy of the file will be created using the new file name and will appear in the PowerPoint window.

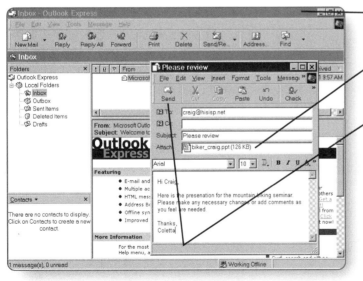

6. **Open** your favorite **e-mail program**.

7. **Attach** the **presentation** to the e-mail message.

8. **Send** the **message** to the designated reviewer.

Commenting on a Presentation

When the reviewer receives a copy of the presentation file, they can begin making the necessary changes and additions. They can edit text, create different color schemes and animations, add graphics, format text, and also place comments on slides.

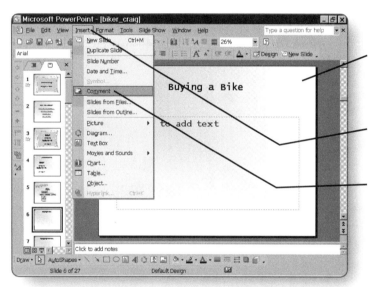

Adding Comments

1. Open the **slide** to which you want to add a comment. The slide will appear in Normal view.

2. Click on **Insert**. The Insert menu will appear.

3. Click on **Comment**. A yellow comment box will appear at the upper-left corner of the slide and the Reviewing toolbar will also appear.

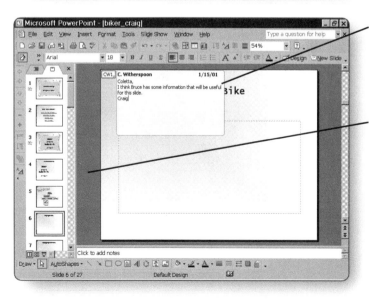

4. Type any **comments**. The comments will appear inside the box and are preceded by your initials and name.

5. Click outside the **comment box**. Your comments will be added to the presentation and will appear as a small comment box containing your initials.

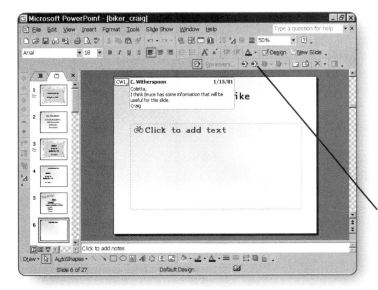

Navigating between Comments

You don't need to look through each slide in a presentation to view all of the comments that have been added to a presentation. Use the Reviewing toolbar to make this task easier.

1. Click on the **Next Item button**. The next slide in the presentation that contains a comment will appear and the comment will be displayed.

2. Click on the **Previous Item button**. The previous slide that contains a comment will appear. When you get to the first and last comments in a presentation, a dialog box opens and asks if you want to continue through the presentation again, or if you want to cancel.

NOTE

When the reviewer is finished with the presentation, the reviewer should save the file and e-mail it back to the original author.

Incorporating Reviewers' Changes

Once the reviewers have finished with their review files, you need to collect their comments and edits and incorporate them into the original presentation file.

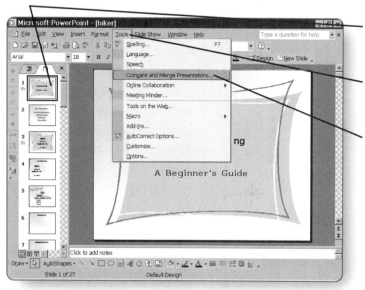

1. **Open** the **original presentation**.

2. **Click** on **Tools**. The Tools menu will appear.

3. **Click** on **Compare and Merge Presentations**. The Choose Files to Merge with Current Presentation dialog box will open.

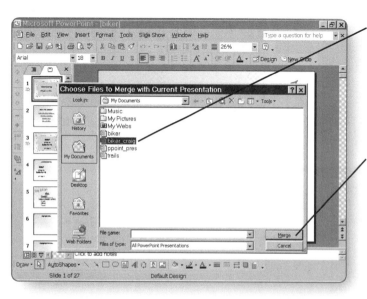

4. **Click** on the **reviewed presentation**. This is the presentation that you want to compare to the original presentation. The review copy will be selected.

5. **Click** on **Merge**. A confirmation dialog box will open.

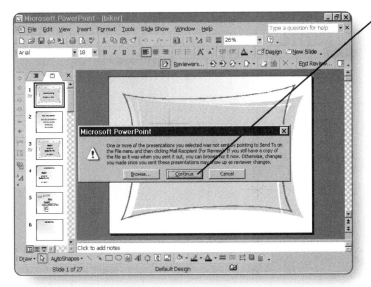

6. **Click** on **Continue**. The Revisions Pane will appear showing all of the changes made by the reviewer.

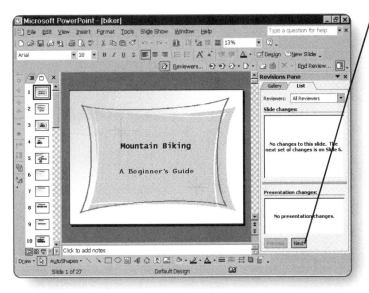

7. **Click** on the **Next button** until you get to a slide that contains changes.

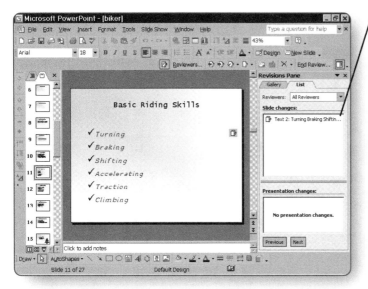

8. **Click** on a **list marker** in the Slide changes list. The change marker on the slide will appear and show the changes made by the reviewer.

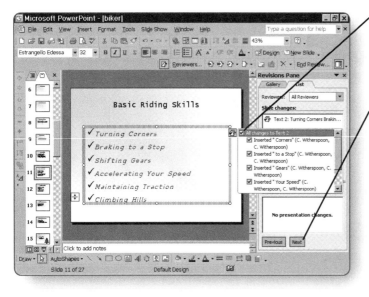

9. **Click** in the **check box** next to the reviewer changes that you want to accept. The changes will be made on the slide.

10. **Click** on **Next** until you find another change. When you are finished, save the file.

11. **Compare** the **original presentation** with the copies you made for any other reviewers by repeating steps 1 through 10.

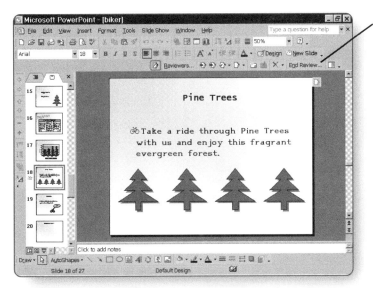

12. Click on **End Review** when you have finished checking all the review copies with the original document. A confirmation dialog box will appear.

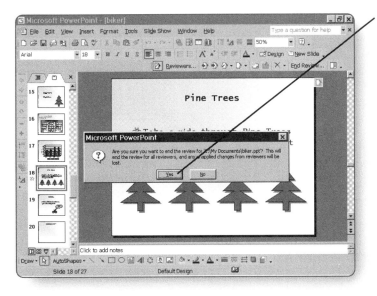

13. Click on **Yes**. All of the review changes will be applied to the presentation file.

NOTE

If reviewers added comments to slides, those comments will be retained in the original file.

16

Adding the Final Touches to Your Presentation

You've finished creating the presentation. It's now time to add a few items that will help you when you deliver your presentation. If you'll be delivering the presentation in front of an audience, you'll want to use notes. You'll also need to practice. To help answer potential questions from the audience, you may want to hide a few slides up your sleeve. Self-running presentations (such as kiosks) that use voice-over narration are more effective than those without accompanying sounds. In this chapter, you'll learn how to:

- Use hidden slides to your advantage
- Rehearse and set timings
- Narrate a presentation

Using Notes

When you're giving a presentation, cue cards are handy item. They not only help relieve anxiety caused by stage fright, they also enhance a presentation. You can develop notes and print them with a copy of the slide. You can use the notes to help keep your presentation on course. To provide an audience with more information, print a notes page that your audience can take home.

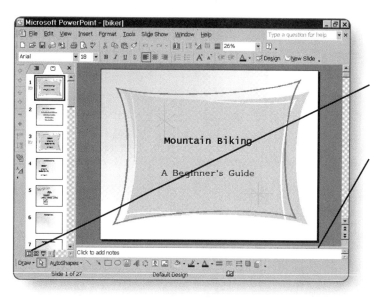

Adding Notes to a Slide

1. **Click** on the **Normal View button**. Your slide will appear in Normal view.

2. **Click** and **drag** the **bar** up to the middle between the Slide pane and the Notes pane. The mouse pointer will turn into a double arrow, and an outline of the bar will show how the pane size will be changed.

3. **Release** the **mouse button**. The two panes will be resized, and you'll have more room with which to work in the Notes pane.

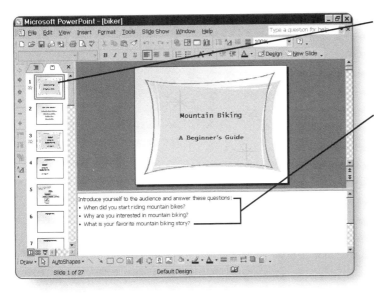

4. Display the **slide** to which you want to add the notes. The slide will appear in the Slide pane.

5. Click inside the **Notes pane** and **type notes** as desired. These notes can be anything that will help you remember what you need to say, or provide additional background if it is needed during the presentation.

TIP

When a presentation is displayed as Web pages, notes can be shown on a page along with the corresponding slide.

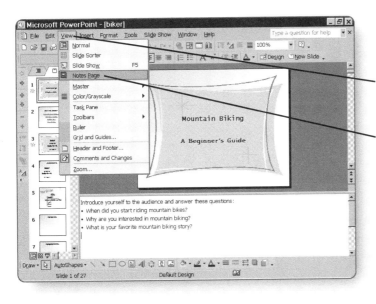

Using Images with Your Notes

1. Click on **View**. The View menu will appear.

2. Click on **Notes Page**. The Notes page for the slide will appear. This is actually a preview of what the Notes page will look like when printed.

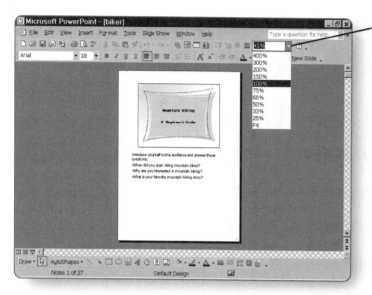

3. **Click** on the **down arrow** next to the Zoom button and select a magnification level. You may want to see the notes section of the Notes page better.

TIP
You can also format the text in the notes section.

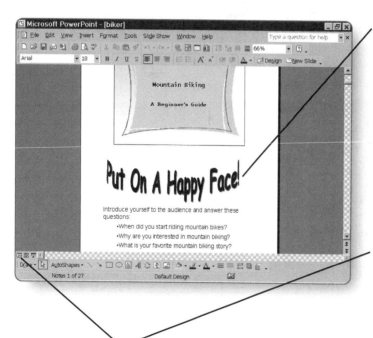

4. **Insert** an **image** or other object into the notes section. You can add any item to the notes section, as you can to a slide. Part III, "Jazzing Up the Presentation," showed you how to insert clip art, pictures stored on your computer, drawing objects, tables, and charts into a slide. You can do the same on the Notes page.

5. **Click** on the **Normal View button**. The selected slide will appear in the Normal view. You won't see the images that you added to the Notes page in the Notes pane.

Working with the Notes Master

You worked with the Slide Master in Chapter 6, "Customizing the Presentation." Like the Slide Master, the Notes Master is where you can set the basic format and look for all the Notes pages in your presentation.

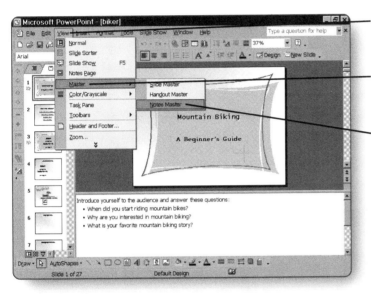

1. Click on **View**. The View menu will appear.

2. Click on **Master**. A submenu will appear.

3. Click on **Notes Master**. The Notes Master page will appear. There are six different elements on the Notes Master that you can change: Header, Date, Notes Body, Footer and Number areas, and you can also change the size of the slide.

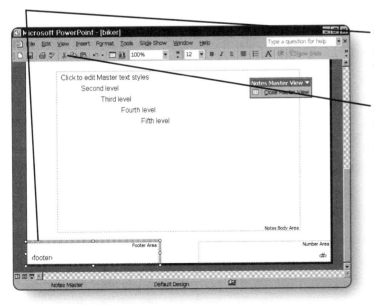

4. To remove an area from the Notes Master, **click** on the **area**. The area will be selected.

5. Click on the **Cut button**. The area will not appear on the Notes pages.

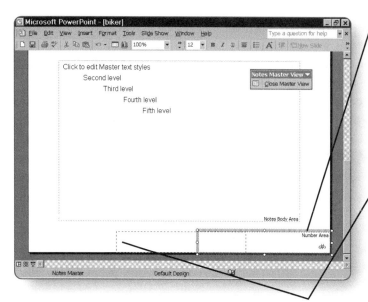

6. To move an area, select the area and then **click** and **drag** the **mouse pointer** to the location where you want to place the area. The mouse pointer will turn into a four-pointed arrowhead and an outline of the area will show you the selected position.

7. **Release** the **mouse button**. The area will move to the new location.

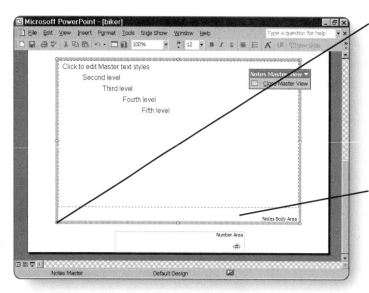

8. To change the size of an area box (including the slide), **click** on the **area** to select it, and **click** and **drag** an **image handle** in the direction that you want to size the area. The mouse pointer will turn into a double arrow, and an outline will show the new size.

9. **Release** the **mouse button**. The area box will be resized.

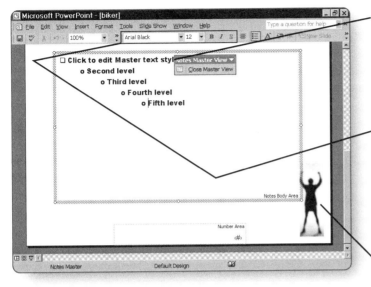

10. To apply new text styles to the text that appears on the Notes pages, **select** the **text** that you want to reformat. The text will be highlighted.

11. Apply the desired formatting **changes**. You can change the font style and size, as well as add attributes like bold and italic.

> **TIP**
>
> If you want an image, such as a company logo, to appear on all the Notes pages, insert the logo onto the Notes Master.

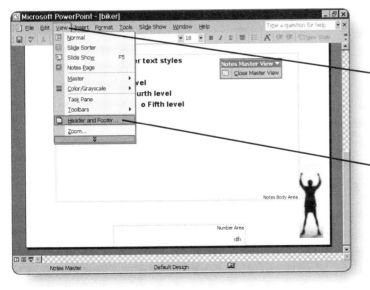

Editing Headers and Footers

1. Click on **View** to add information to the Header and Footer areas. The View menu will appear.

2. Click on **Header and Footer**. The Header and Footer dialog box will open, and the Notes and Handouts tab will be on top.

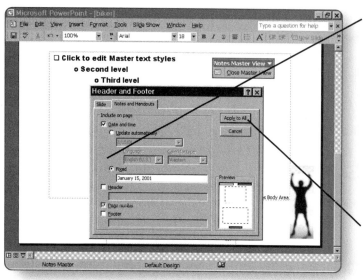

3. **Place** a **check mark** in the check boxes next to those header and footer items that you want to appear on the Notes pages. Type any text that you want to appear in those areas. You can also specify the information to appear in the Date Area of the header and the Number Area of the footer.

4. **Click** on **Apply to All**. The information you typed will appear in the Header and Footer areas.

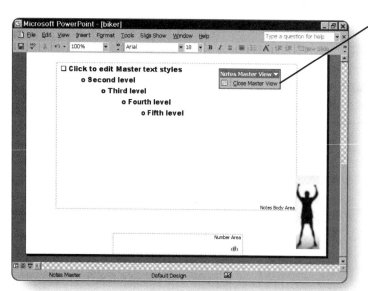

5. **Click** on the **Close Master View button** on the Notes Master View toolbar when you finish making changes to the Notes Master. You will return to the view you were using previously.

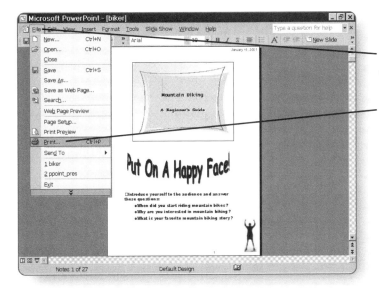

Printing Your Notes

1. **Click** on **File**. The File menu will appear.

2. **Click** on **Print**. The Print dialog box will open.

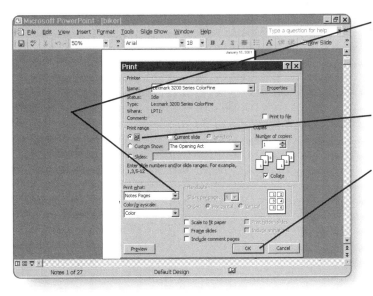

3. **Click** on the **down arrow** next to the Print what list box and **click** on **Notes Pages**. The option will appear in the list box.

4. **Change** any other **options** as needed.

5. **Click** on **OK**. The Notes pages will be printed.

Using Hidden Slides

Sometime during a presentation, you'll probably receive questions from your audience. Before you deliver your presentation, try to anticipate some of the questions you'll be asked. Make slides that will answer the questions, or provide additional background information in the notes. Your audience will think that you're brilliant!

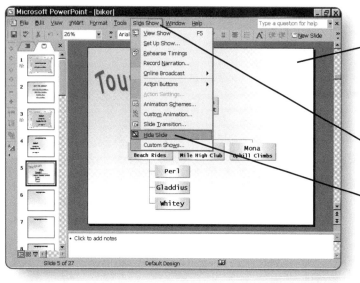

Hiding a Slide

1. **Display** the **slide** that you want hidden in the Normal view. The slide will appear in the Normal view.

2. **Click** on **Slide Show**. The Slide Show menu will appear.

3. **Click** on **Hide Slide**. The slide will be hidden until you ask for it during your slide show.

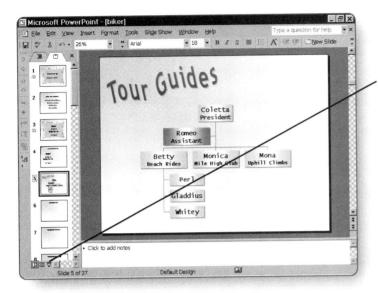

Using Hidden Slides during a Slide Show

1. **Click** on the **Slide Show button**. A slide show of the screens in your presentation will begin.

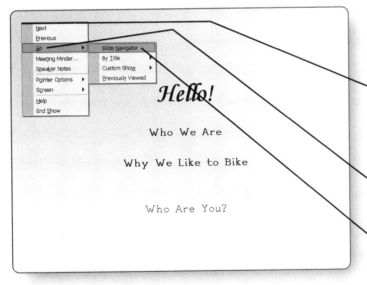

2. **Move** through the **slide show**. The presentation slides will display in the Slide Show.

3. When you want to display a hidden slide, **right-click** on the **slide** that is showing. A shortcut menu will appear.

4. **Click** on **Go**. A submenu will appear.

5. **Click** on **Slide Navigator**. The Slide Navigator dialog box will open.

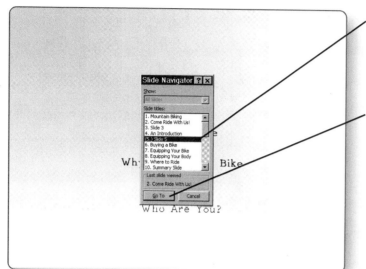

6. **Click** on the **hidden slide** that you want to view. A number in parenthesis indicates a hidden slide. The slide will be selected.

7. **Click** on the **Go To button**. The hidden slide will appear during the slide show.

Rehearsing for the Slide Show

Practice, practice, practice. Be prepared. These and other sayings that we heard repeatedly in our younger years are still good advice today. One way to make sure that your presentation fits within an allotted time frame is to set timings to each slide. You have two choices: 1) you can go through the list of slides and set an amount of time that each slide will display, applying a specific amount of time to a single slide or group of slides; 2) you can set the slide timing while you rehearse the slide show.

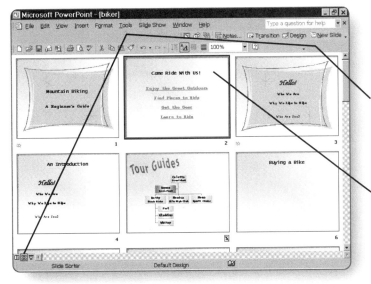

Applying Slide Show Timing to Selected Slides

1. **Click** on the **Slide Sorter View button**. The presentation will appear in the Slide Sorter view.

2. **Select** the **slides** to which you want to set the timing. The slides will be selected.

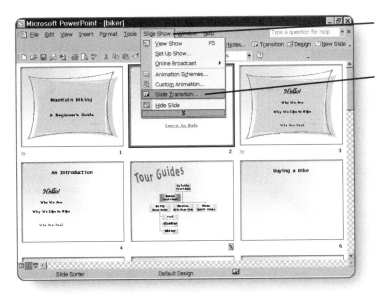

3. **Click** on **Slide Show**. The Slide Show menu will appear.

4. **Click** on **Slide Transition**. The Slide Transition task pane will open.

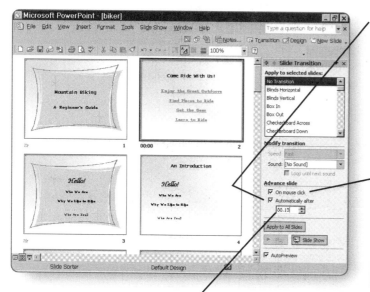

5. Click in the **Automatically after check box**. A check mark will appear in the box, and the time in the text box will be selected.

TIP

To preserve the ability to advance through a slide show using the mouse, leave the check mark in the On mouse click check box.

---

6. Type the **number** of minutes or seconds that you want the slide to display on the screen before the next screen appears.

7. Close the **Task Pane** when you have finished setting the amount of time each slide should display before moving on to the next slide. The timing will be applied to the selected slides.

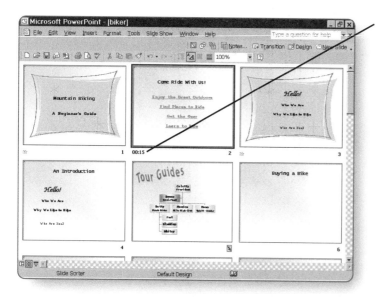

You'll notice that the timing appears below the slide. If you want to change this timing, right-click on the slide and select Slide Transition from the shortcut menu that appears.

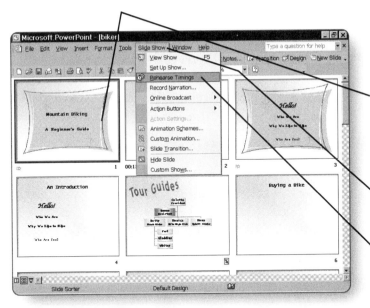

Setting the Timing While You Rehearse

1. **Click** on the first **slide** that you want to appear when you start the slide show. The slide will be selected.

2. **Click** on **Slide Show**. The Slide Show menu will appear.

3. **Click** on **Rehearse Timings**. The slide show will start with the selected slide, and the Rehearsal toolbar will appear on the screen.

4. **Practice** your **delivery** for the first slide.

5. When you have finished with the first slide, **click** on the **Next button** on the Rehearsal toolbar. The time spent on the first slide will be recorded, and PowerPoint will begin tracking the timing for the second slide.

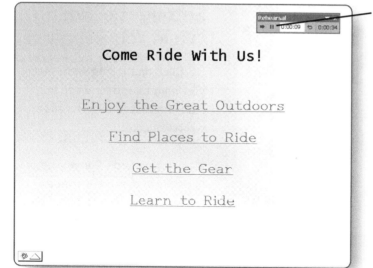

6. **Click** on the **Pause button** if you need to take a break from the rehearsal. The timer will stop until you are ready to begin again.

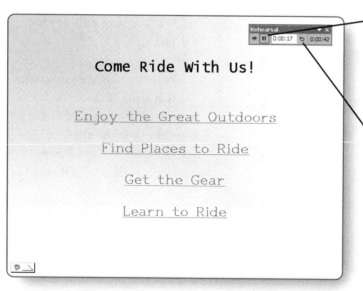

7. **Click** again on the **Pause button**. The time will begin recording at the place where you left off.

TIP

If you want to erase the time spent on a slide and start the timing over for the slide, click on the Repeat button. The time counter will be cleared, and you can start over with the rehearsal for the slide.

8. Click on the **Close button** on the Rehearsal toolbar when you finish rehearsing the last slide. The slide show will close, and a confirmation dialog box will open.

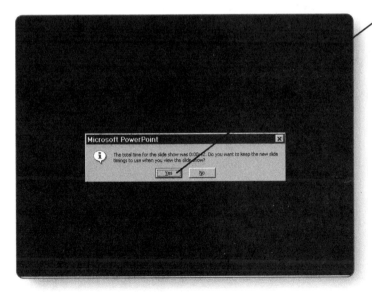

9. Click on **Yes**. Your timings will be applied to each slide in the presentation.

Adding Voice-over Narration

Voice-over narration works great in presentations for which a live speaker will not be present. If the presentation will be used on the Internet or your company intranet, narration can take the place of the speaker. You might also want to record the actual presentation so that you have a permanent record. If you will be showing the presentation in a kiosk (on an unattended computer that runs a presentation on a continuous basis), you might want to consider narration.

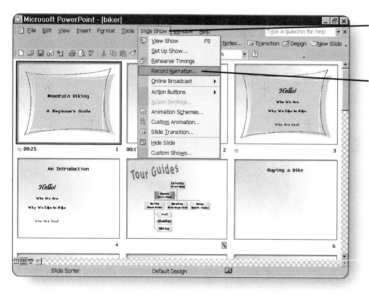

1. **Click** on **Slide Show**. The Slide Show menu will appear.

2. **Click** on **Record Narration**. The Record Narration dialog box will open. Be sure to make a note of your free disk space and how long you can record.

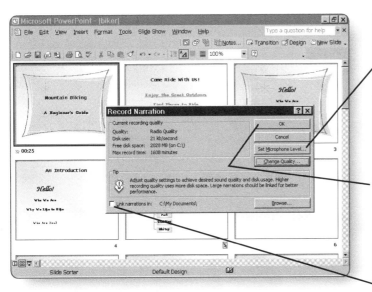

NOTE

If this is the first time you'll be using this feature, click on the Set Microphone Level button and follow the wizard instructions.

3. Click on **OK**. The slide show will start and you can begin recording.

TIP

You can link the narration to the presentation file. Place a check in the Link narrations in check box. Change the location of the narration file by clicking on the Browse button.

4. Work your **way** through the presentation until you come to the end of the presentation. The screen will go black, and a confirmation dialog box will appear.

TIP

You can pause the narration. Right-click on a slide show screen and select Pause Narration. Start again by right-clicking and selecting Resume Narration.

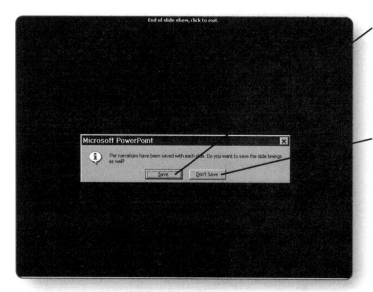

5a. **Click** on **Save**. The timing of the slide show will be saved along with the narration.

OR

5b. **Click** on **Don't Save**. Only the narration will be saved.

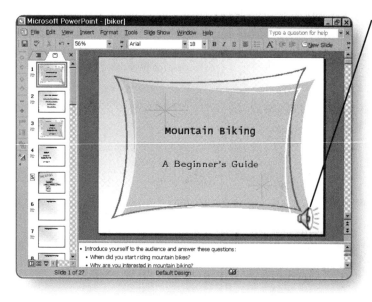

You'll see a sound icon located at the bottom-right corner of each slide. To listen to the narration, double-click on the icon.

17

Printing the Presentation

When you first started building your presentation, you probably had a good idea how you wanted to deliver it. You probably told the AutoContent wizard just how you wanted to do this. Even if you set up a presentation one way, this doesn't mean that you can't change your mind later. Or maybe you need multiple options for delivering the presentation. In this chapter, you'll learn how to:

- Change a color presentation to grayscale
- Create handouts

Printing in Black and White

You've created a great-looking presentation, in color of course, and now you need to distribute paper copies. If you can only print your presentation in black and white, you'll still want your presentation to look good. PowerPoint will automatically convert your presentation to grayscale. You can then go through and adjust any images that may not print clearly.

NOTE

When you convert a color picture to grayscale, the darkest areas of the picture will be black, lighter colors will turn to shades of gray (depending on the darkness of the color), and areas of white or very pale color will contain no color.

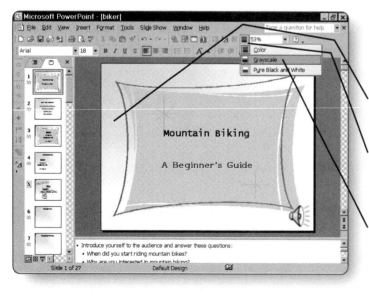

Converting Color Slides into Grayscale

1. **Open** the **presentation** in Normal view.

2. **Click** on the **Color/Grayscale button** on the Standard toolbar. A menu will appear.

3. **Click** on **Grayscale**. The displayed slide will turn from color to various shades of gray. Scroll through the slides and look for grayscale images that don't appear properly on the screen.

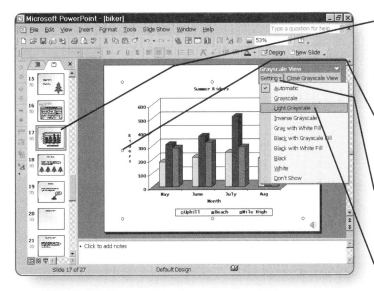

4. Navigate to a **slide** that contains an object that doesn't appear correctly. The slide will display in the Normal view.

5. Click on the **object** that you want to adjust. The object will be selected.

6. Click on **Setting** on the Grayscale View toolbar. A submenu will appear.

7. Click on an **option** to change the color of the selected object. If an image is too dark and you want to lighten it, select Light Grayscale or Inverse Grayscale. The selected command will be applied to the object.

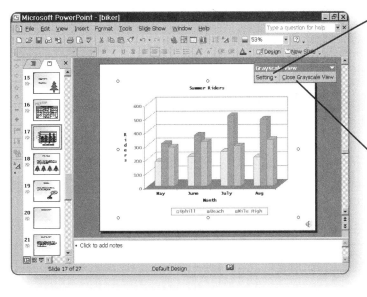

8. If you do not like the enhancement that was made to the image, **click** on the Setting button to open the **Setting menu** and select a different option.

9. Click on the **Close Grayscale View button** when you have finished making changes. Your presentation slides are now ready to be printed on a black and white printer.

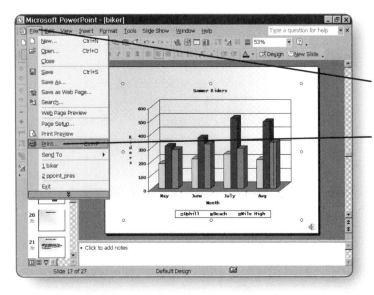

Printing Slides in Grayscale

1. **Click** on **File**. The File menu will appear.

2. **Click** on **Print**. The Print dialog box will open.

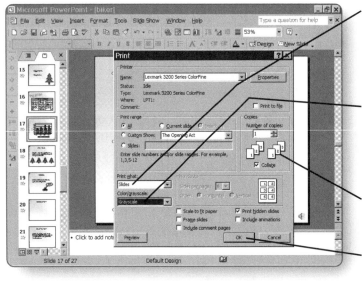

3. **Click** the **down arrow** next to the Print what list box and **click** on **Slides**. The option will appear in the list box.

4. **Click** the **down arrow** next to the Color/grayscale list box and **click** on **Grayscale**. The option will appear in the list box.

5. **Change** other **options** as needed.

6. **Click** on **OK**. The slides will print.

NOTE

The changes made to an image in the Grayscale Preview mode have no effect on the original color of the image.

Creating Handouts

One way to help guide your audience through a presentation is to provide them with handouts that contain pictures of the various slides in the slide show.

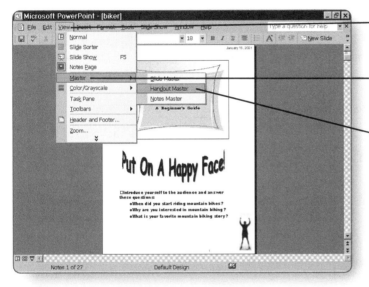

1. Click on **View**. The View menu will appear.

2. Click on **Master**. A submenu will appear.

3. Click on **Handout Master**. The Handout Master will appear. The Handout Master can help you decide how you want the printed pages to appear.

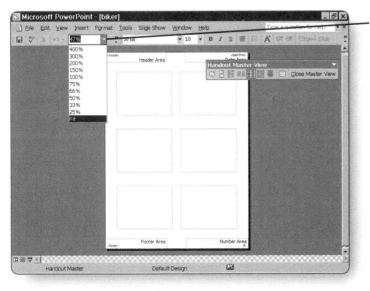

4. Click on the **down arrow** next to the Zoom list box and **click** on **Fit to view the entire page on your screen**. The entire page will appear.

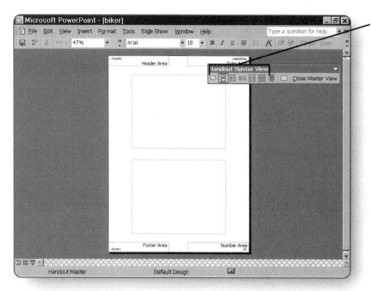

5. **Click** on a **button** on the Handout Master View toolbar. You will have the option to print one, two, three, four, six, or nine slides per page. You can also use this view to print an outline of the presentation. The number of slides that will appear on the Handout pages will change.

TIP

To change the look of the Handout Master, you can change the various elements on the Handout Master just as you can with the Slide and Notes Masters.

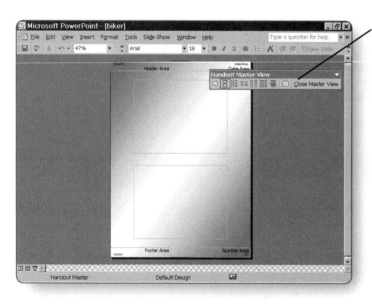

6. **Click** on the **Close Master View button** on the Handout Master View toolbar when you have decided on the look you want to use for your handouts. The presentation will appear in the previous view in which you were working.

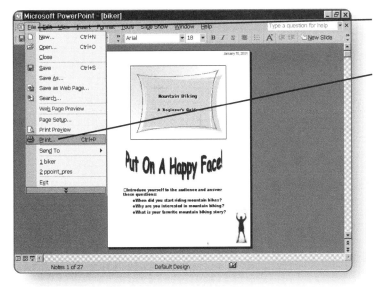

7. Click on **File**. The File menu will appear.

8. Click on **Print**. The Print dialog box will open.

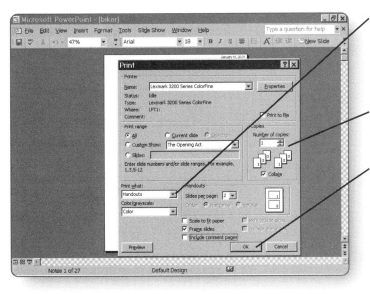

9. Click the **down arrow** next to the Print what list box and **click** on **Handouts**. The option will appear in the list box.

10. Change any other **options** as needed.

11. Click on **OK**. The handouts will be printed.

18

Delivering the Presentation

You're ready to give your presentation in front of a live audience. Each slide contains just the right content and is formatted so that your audience can see each slide clearly. You've rehearsed and rehearsed until your voice is hoarse. Your handouts are printed and stashed away in your briefcase. Now it's time to prepare the presentation file before you hit the road. In this chapter, you'll learn how to:

- Pack a presentation so that it can be set up on different computers
- Set up a presentation for a speaker
- Give your audience control of the presentation
- Run an unattended presentation in a kiosk

Embedding Fonts

Not all computers have the same set of fonts installed, which means that your presentation may not display the same when viewed on another computer. Here's how to embed fonts into a presentation to ensure that the presentation displays the same on each computer that runs it. Keep in mind that embedding fonts will increase the file size.

1. Open the **presentation file**. The presentation slides will appear in PowerPoint.

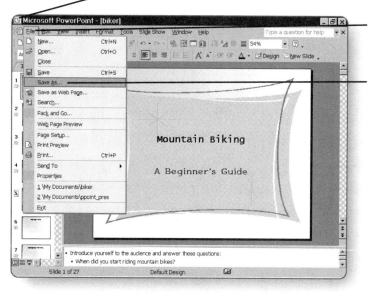

2. Click on **File**. The File menu will appear.

3. Click on **Save As**. The Save As dialog box will appear.

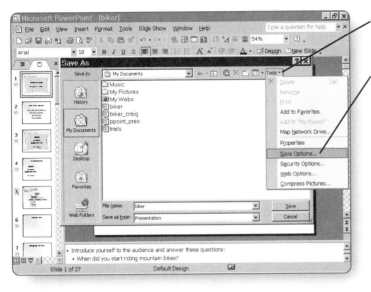

4. Click on **Tools**. The Tools menu will appear.

5. Click on **Save Options**. The Save Options dialog box will open.

6. Click in the **Embed TrueType fonts check box**. A check mark will appear in the check box.

7a. Click the **Embed characters in use only option button** if the presentation will only be viewed on the other computer. The option will be selected.

OR

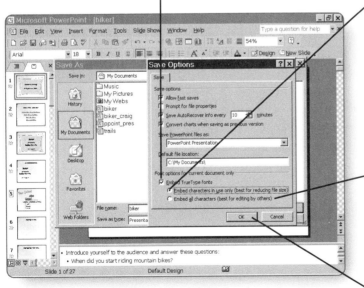

7b. Click on the **Embed all characters option button** if the presentation will be edited on the other computer. The option will be selected.

8. Click on **OK**. The dialog box will close and you will be returned to the Save As dialog box.

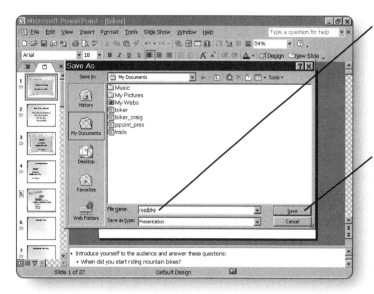

9. **Click** in the **File name text box** and **type** a different **file name** for the presentation. A separate presentation with embedded fonts will be created in a new file.

10. **Click** on **Save**. The presentation will be saved with the embedded fonts.

Using the Pack and Go Wizard

If you'll be displaying the presentation on a variety of computers, you'll want to consider using the Pack and Go wizard. The Pack and Go wizard can make a copy of your presentation along with a viewer, the fonts, and any linked files, to a diskette, CD-ROM, or network drive. No matter which computer you use to display the presentation, it will look as you originally formatted it. You don't even need to worry if the computer you will use has the appropriate programs or viewers to display the presentation. Your presentation is a self-contained traveling show.

Packing a Presentation

1. **Open** the **presentation**. The presentation slides will appear in PowerPoint.

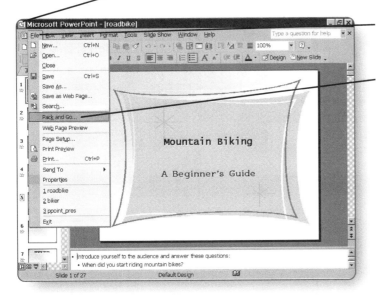

2. **Click** on **File**. The File menu will appear.

3. **Click** on **Pack and Go**. The Pack and Go wizard will open, and the Start page of the wizard will appear.

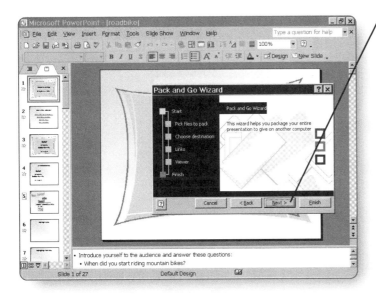

4. **Click** on **Next**. The Pick files to pack page of the wizard will appear.

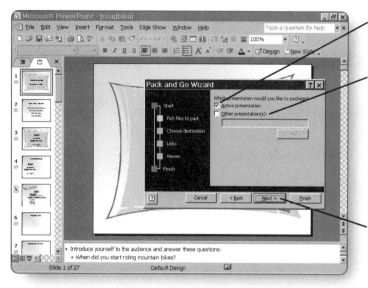

5. Place a **check mark** in the Active presentation check box.

6. If you want to pack other presentations along with the open presentation, **click** in the **Other presentation(s) check box** and type the path and filename of the other presentations.

7. Click on **Next**. The Choose destination page of the wizard will appear.

8a. Click on **the A:\ drive option button** to save the presentation to a floppy disk. The option will be selected.

OR

NOTE

If you pack your presentation onto floppy disks, you may need more than one disk.

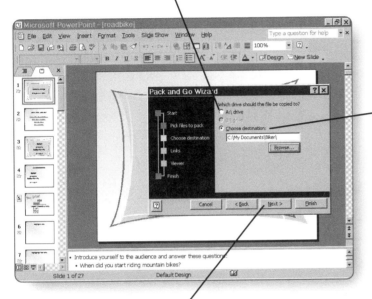

8b. To save the presentation to another location (such as a folder on the computer or a network location), **click** on the **Choose destination option button** and type the directory path where you want to store the packed presentation.

9. Click on **Next**. The Links page of the wizard will display.

NOTE

If a Zip drive is attached to the computer, the drive designation for the Zip drive will also appear as an option.

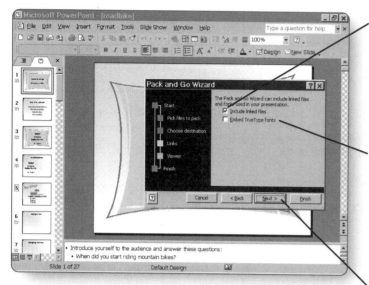

10. Click in the **Include linked files check box** to add to the packed presentation any files that are linked to the presentation. A check will appear in the box.

11. Click in the **Embed True Type fonts check box** if you want any fonts that you applied to text to be packed with the presentation. A check mark will appear in the box.

12. Click on **Next**. The Viewer page of the wizard will appear.

13a. **Click** on the **Don't include the Viewer option button** if the person who will be unpacking and looking at the presentation has PowerPoint and does not need a separate viewer to see the presentation. The option will be selected.

OR

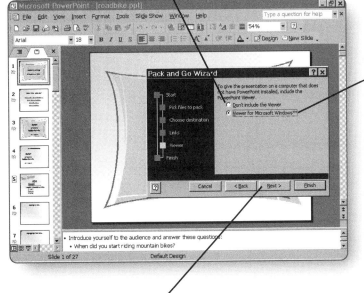

13b. **Click** on the **Viewer for Microsoft Windows option button** if the person will need a means for viewing the presentation. The option will be selected.

14. **Click** on **Next**. The Finish page of the wizard will appear.

NOTE

If you do not have the PowerPoint viewer installed on your computer, you won't see the Viewer for Microsoft Windows option button, but an option to obtain the viewer will appear on the wizard screen. Click on the Download the Viewer button to connect to the Internet and the Microsoft Web site. Follow the instructions to download and install the viewer.

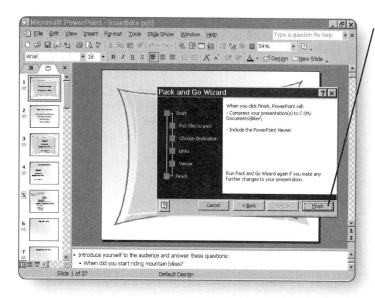

15. **Click** on **Finish**. The Pack and Go Status dialog box will open, and your presentation will be packed away to the destination you specified. You're now ready to pass that presentation along to others for their viewing pleasure.

Unpacking a Presentation

1a. **Insert** the **disk** or **CD** onto which you packed the presentation into the computer where you want to unpack the presentation. The disk or CD will be in the drive.

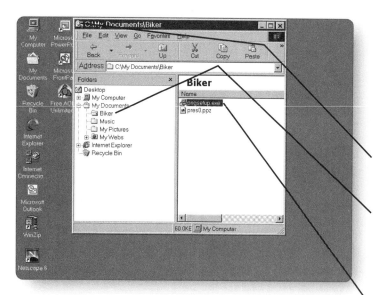

OR

1b. **Connect** to the **network** where the packed presentation is stored. A connection to the network will be made.

2. **Open Windows Explorer**. Windows Explorer will appear.

3. **Navigate** to the **drive** and **folder** where the packed presentation is located. The drive and folder will be selected.

4. **Double-click** on the **file** named pngsetup.exe. The Pack and Go Setup dialog box will open.

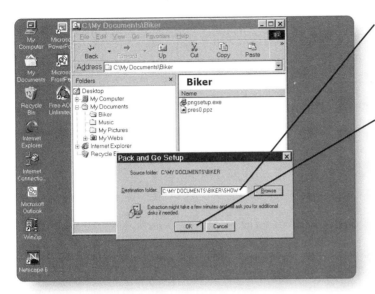

5. **Type** the **drive** and **path** where you want to store the presentation in the Destination folder text box.

6. **Click** on **OK**. The presentation will unpack to the specified directory. When the process is finished, a confirmation dialog box will open.

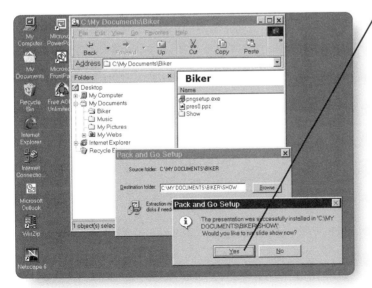

7. **Click** on **Yes**. The presentation will open in PowerPoint or in the viewer.

TIP

You can run the slide show at a later time. Just open the folder where you unpacked the presentation. Right-click on the presentation (it's the one with the .ppt extension) and click on Show.

Using a Speaker to Deliver a Presentation

Okay, it's time to take a deep breath and get ready to deliver your presentation. Imagine that your audience members are sitting in front of you in their underwear, or maybe they are wearing funny hats. Whatever technique you use, relax before you start the show. Then, once you've got your nerve up, set up PowerPoint to run the slide show and let the show begin!

1. **Open** the **presentation file** in PowerPoint.

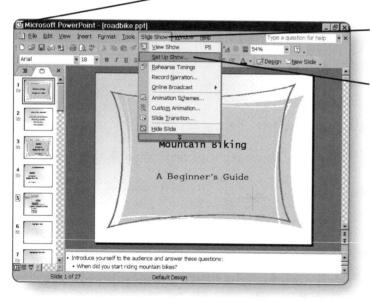

2. **Click** on **Slide Show**. The Slide Show menu will appear.

3. **Click** on **Set Up Show**. The Set Up Show dialog box will open.

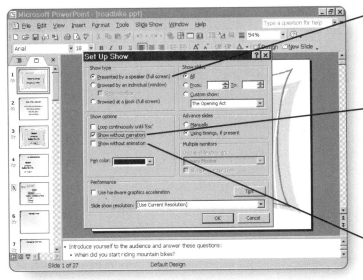

4. **Click** on the **Presented by a speaker (full screen) option button**. The option will be selected.

5. **Click** in the **Show without narration check box** if you added narration to the presentation but do not wish to use it. A check mark will appear in the box.

6. **Click** in the **Show without animation check box** if you applied slide transitions or animations and do not want to display them in the presentation. A check mark will appear in the box.

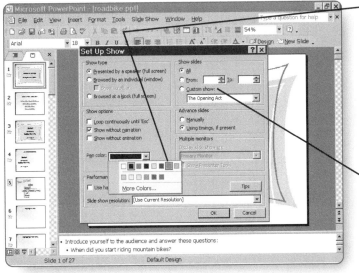

7. If you use the pen to draw on slides during the show and want to change the pen color, **click** the **down arrow** next to the Pen color list box and **click** on a **color**. The color will appear in the list box.

NOTE

You don't have to use all of a presentation all the time. Select a group of slides in a presentation to use as a slide show. You learned how to create custom shows in Chapter 6, "Customizing the Presentation."

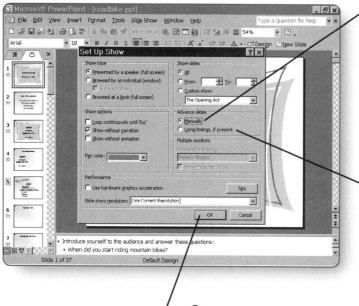

8a. **Click** on the **Manually option button** if you want the speaker to click on a slide in order to advance to the next slide. The option will be selected.

OR

8b. **Click** on the **Using timings, if present option button** to have the presentation use the timings that you set to advance through the slides. The option will be selected.

9. **Click** on **OK**. Start the slide show by clicking on the Slide Show button or by pressing the F5 key.

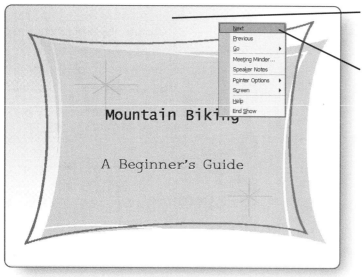

10. **Right-click** on the **slide show**. A menu will appear.

11. **Click** on a **slide show control**.

Allowing an Audience to Browse a Presentation

You may want to give your audience the leisure of running the slide show at their convenience. Before you make a copy of the presentation, set it up so that it will be easy to view.

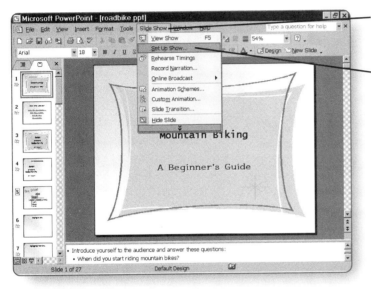

1. **Click** on **Slide Show**. The Slide Show menu will appear.

2. **Click** on **Set Up Show**. The Set Up Show dialog box will open.

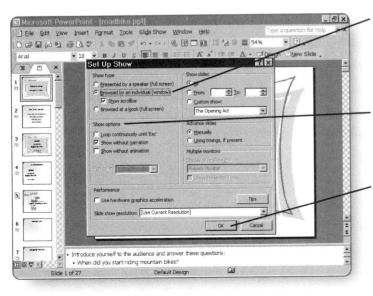

3. **Click** on the **Browsed by an individual (window) option button**. The option will be selected.

4. **Change** any other **options** as needed. The options will be selected.

5. **Click** on **OK**. When you run the slide show, the presentation will appear in a viewer window.

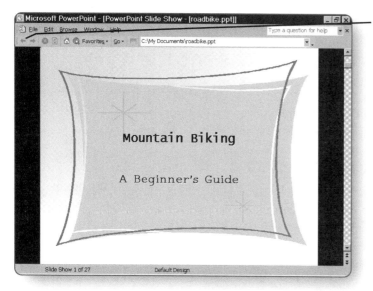

The viewer contains controls for moving back and forth in a presentation, copying slides, printing, and accessing the Internet.

Setting Up a Self-Running Presentation

You may have seen kiosks at department store beauty counters that show how to apply makeup and tie pretty hair ribbons. You also may have seen small monitors in hardware stores that showcase the latest in power tools. If you'd like your presentation to run unattended, make sure the presentation is equipped with automatic slide timings (see Chapter 16, "Adding the Final Touches"), then save it as a PowerPoint Show file so that it always opens as a slide show.

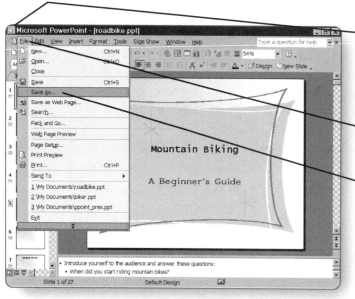

1. **Open** the **presentation** that you want to run in kiosk mode. The presentation slides will appear in PowerPoint.

2. **Click** on **File**. The File menu will appear.

3. **Click** on **Save As**. The Save As dialog box will open.

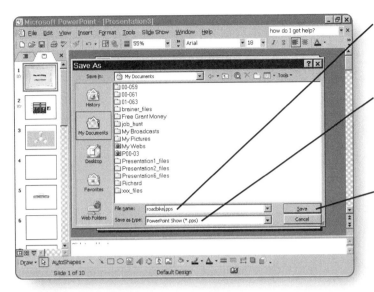

4. **Click** in the **File name text box** and **type** a **name** for the kiosk slideshow.

5. **Click** the **Save as type drop-down list button** and **select PowerPoint Show (*.pps)** from the list.

6. **Click** on **Save**. The presentation file will be saved as a PowerPoint self-running show.

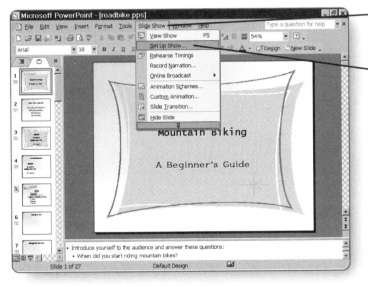

7. **Click** on **Slide Show**. The Slide Show menu will appear.

8. **Click** on **Set Up Show**. The Set Up Show dialog box will open.

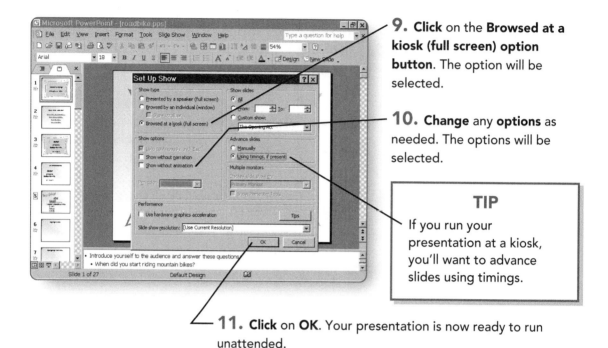

9. **Click** on the **Browsed at a kiosk (full screen) option button**. The option will be selected.

10. **Change** any **options** as needed. The options will be selected.

TIP

If you run your presentation at a kiosk, you'll want to advance slides using timings.

11. **Click** on **OK**. Your presentation is now ready to run unattended.

19

Publishing the Presentation on the Web

One way to share your presentation with a large number of people who may be scattered over a large area is to publish it on the World Wide Web. Before you publish your presentation, you may want to add a few Web elements, such as hyperlinks. If your audience is familiar with browsing the Internet, these additions will make it easier for them to navigate through the presentation. In this chapter, you'll learn how to:

- Make a GIF image from a slide
- Create hyperlinks and other navigation controls
- Get your presentation ready for the Web
- Publish your Web presentation

Turning a Slide into a GIF Image

A popular file format used on the Internet for graphics is GIF (or Graphics Interchange Format). GIF images work well on Web pages; all browsers can display GIF files. Their small file size makes them a good choice for e-mail attachments. If recipients use an e-mail program that displays HTML format, they can view the GIF file from their mail program.

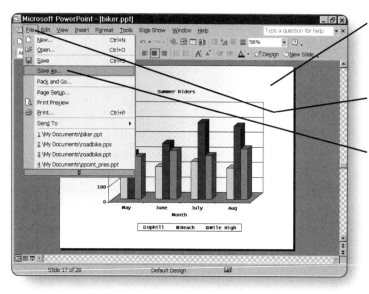

1. **Open** the **slide** that you want to save as a GIF image. The slide will appear in the Normal view.

2. **Click** on **File**. The File menu will appear.

3. **Click** on **Save As**. The Save As dialog box will open.

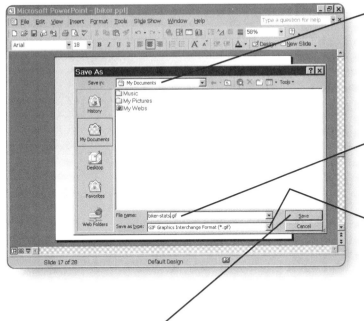

4. **Click** on the **down arrow** next to the Save in list box, and **click** on the **folder** in which you want to store the GIF file. The folder will appear in the Save in list box.

5. **Click** in the **File name text box** and **type** a **name** for the GIF file.

6. **Click** on the **down arrow** next to the Save as type list box and **click** on **GIF Graphics Interchange Format**. The option will appear in the list box.

7. **Click** on **Save**. A confirmation dialog box will open.

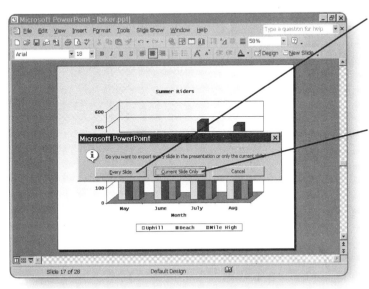

8a. **Click** on **Every Slide**. Each slide in the presentation will be converted to GIF format.

OR

8b. **Click** on **Current Slide Only**. Only the selected slide will be saved in the GIF format.

Designing Navigation Controls

Navigation controls help your audience move around inside your presentation and link to places outside your presentation. These controls can take the form of buttons that move your audience between slides. They can also be text or image hyperlinks that move the audience from slide to slide, or to someplace else on the Web.

Using Action Buttons to Navigate a Presentation

PowerPoint includes a number of navigation controls (called Action buttons) that make moving around a presentation easy. These buttons allow you to go to the first page of the presentation with a single click or move to the next or previous slide in the presentation. You can add navigation controls either to each individual slide or to the Slide Master. Action buttons placed on the Slide Master will appear on each slide.

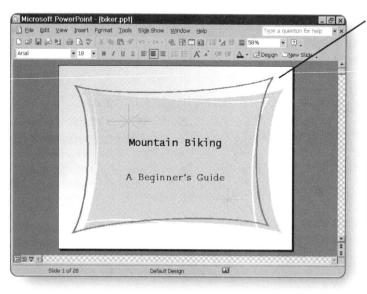

1. **Open** the **slide** on which you want to place the Action buttons. The slide will appear in the Normal view.

NOTE

For help with the Slide Master, see Chapter 6, "Customizing the Presentation."

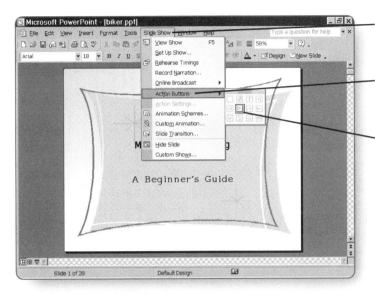

2. **Click** on **Slide Show**. The Slide Show menu will appear.

3. **Click** on **Action Buttons**. A submenu will appear.

4. **Click** on the **button** that you want to insert into the slide. The mouse pointer will turn into a crosshair.

NOTE

The most commonly used navigation buttons are the Home, Back, and Forward buttons.

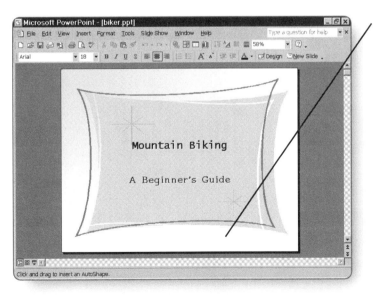

5. **Click** on the **slide** where you want to place the navigation button. The button will appear in a predefined size, and the Action Settings dialog box will open.

TIP

To add an Action button of a different size, click and hold on the side where you want to place the button, drag the mouse pointer until the outline is the size you want, and release the mouse button.

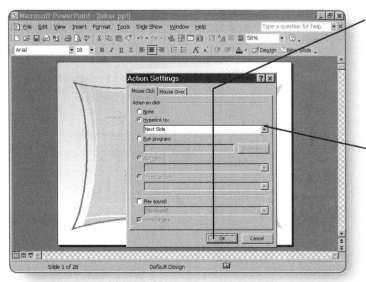

6. **Click** on **OK** to accept the default links. The button will be used as a hyperlink to the specified page.

TIP

If you want to change the slide that the button links to, click the down arrow next to the Hyperlink to list box and select a different slide.

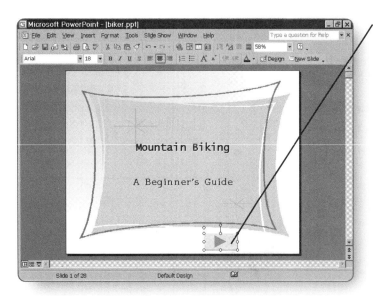

7. **Add** additional **Action buttons** to the slide as needed. The Action buttons will appear on the slide in the selected position.

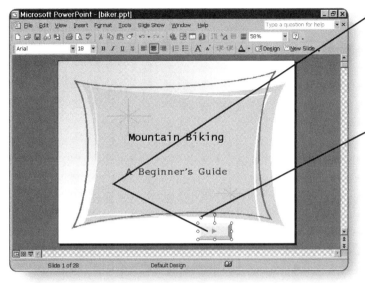

8. Click on the **button** to change the look of an Action button. The button will be selected, and the shape handles will appear.

- Click and drag the adjustment handle to change the bevel depth of the button and the size of the image within the button. Drag the mouse pointer to the left to turn the beveled edge into a single line appearing around the button. Drag the mouse pointer to the right and the beveled edge will become larger.

- Click and drag the resize handles to change the height and width of the Action button.

- Click and drag the rotate handle to change the orientation of the Action button.

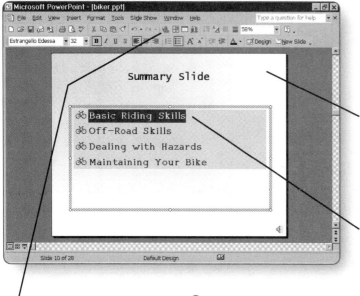

Creating a Hyperlink to Another Slide in the Presentation

1. Open the **slide** onto which you want to place a hyperlink that links to another slide within the presentation. The slide will appear in Normal view.

2. Select the **text** that you want to use as the hyperlink. The text will be selected.

3. Click on the **Insert Hyperlink button**. The Insert Hyperlink dialog box will open.

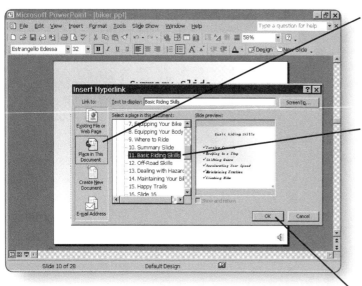

4. Click on the **Place in This Document button** found in the Link to list. A list of slides found in the presentation will appear in the center of the dialog box.

5. Click on the **slide** in the Select a place in this document list box that you want to appear when a visitor clicks on the hyperlink. The slide will be selected, and a preview of the slide will appear in the Slide preview box.

6. Click on **OK**. The hyperlink will be created.

Creating Hyperlinks to Web Sites

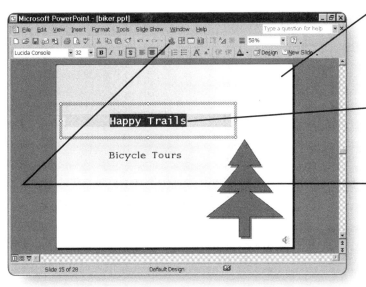

1. **Open** the **slide** into which you want to place the hyperlink. The slide will appear in Normal view.

2. **Select** the **text** or image that will be used as the hyperlink. The text will be selected.

3. **Click** on the **Insert Hyperlink button**. The Insert Hyperlink dialog box will open.

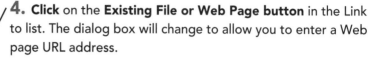

4. Click on the **Existing File or Web Page button** in the Link to list. The dialog box will change to allow you to enter a Web page URL address.

5. Click in the **Address text box** and **type** the **URL address** of the Web page to which you want to create the hyperlink.

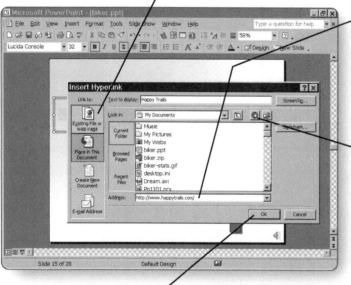

TIP

If you don't know the URL address, and if it's a page you visited recently using your Web browser, click on the Browsed Pages button and select from the list. You can also click on the Browse the Web button and connect to the Internet.

6. Click on **OK**. The hyperlink will be created.

Creating an E-mail Hyperlink

To give your audience an easy way to contact you, place an e-mail hyperlink on one of the slides. When people click on the e-mail hyperlink, a new message window will open from their default e-mail program. Your e-mail address (or any other address you specify) will appear in the To field. They just need to type a message and send it to you.

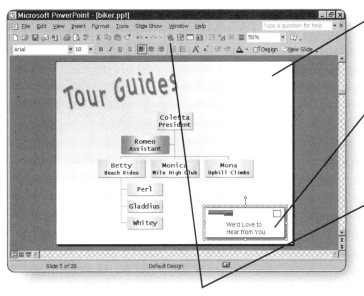

1. **Open** the **page** where you want to place the e-mail hyperlink. The page will appear in Normal view.

2. **Select** the **text or image** that you want to use as the e-mail hyperlink. The item will be selected.

3. **Click** on the **Insert Hyperlink button**. The Insert Hyperlink dialog box will open.

4. **Click** on the **E-mail Address button** in the Link to list.

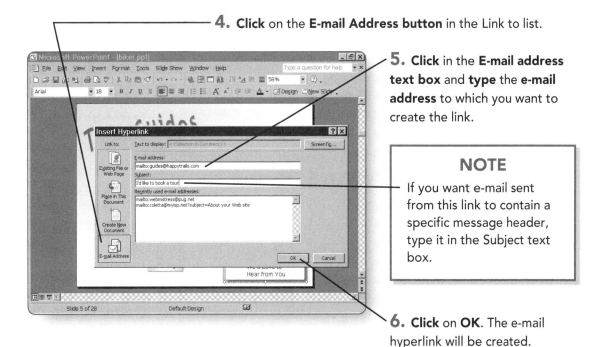

5. **Click** in the **E-mail address text box** and **type** the **e-mail address** to which you want to create the link.

NOTE

If you want e-mail sent from this link to contain a specific message header, type it in the Subject text box.

6. **Click** on **OK**. The e-mail hyperlink will be created.

Adding Special Effects to Hyperlinks

You can add special effects that will appear when the mouse pointer is held over a hyperlink. You can turn a hyperlink a different color and have a sound play.

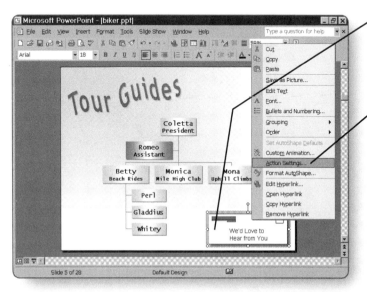

1. **Right-click** on the **hyperlink** to which you want to add the effect. A shortcut menu will appear.

2. **Click** on **Action Settings**. The Action Settings dialog box will open.

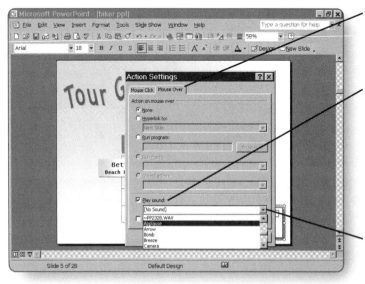

3. **Click** on the **Mouse Over tab**. The Mouse Over tab will move to the front.

4. **Click** in the **Play sound check box** if you want a sound to play when the mouse pointer is held over the hyperlink. A check mark will appear in the box, and you will be able to select from a list of sounds.

5. **Click** on the **down arrow** next to the Play sound list box. A list of sounds will appear.

6. **Click** on a **sound**. The sound will appear in the list box.

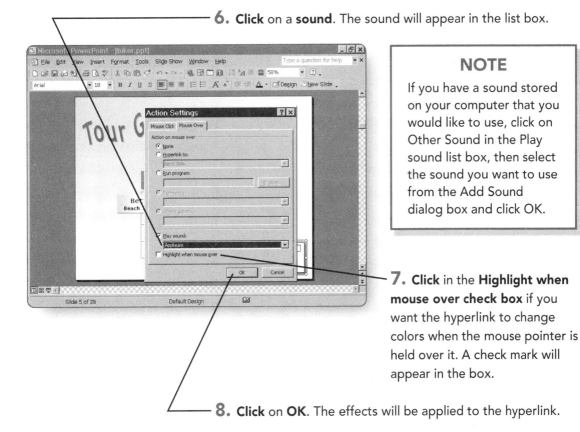

NOTE

If you have a sound stored on your computer that you would like to use, click on Other Sound in the Play sound list box, then select the sound you want to use from the Add Sound dialog box and click OK.

7. **Click** in the **Highlight when mouse over check box** if you want the hyperlink to change colors when the mouse pointer is held over it. A check mark will appear in the box.

8. **Click** on **OK**. The effects will be applied to the hyperlink.

Using the Notes and Outline Panes in a Web Presentation

When you publish a presentation on the Web, the text and images you placed in the Outline and Notes panes will automatically appear as part of the Web presentation. You can use this information to help your audience navigate through your site and find other useful information.

Hiding the Notes and Outlines Panes

If you don't want to use the Notes and Outline panes, you can turn them off. The notes and outline won't appear when your audience views the presentation in a Web browser.

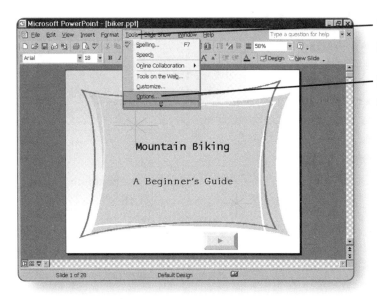

1. **Click** on **Tools**. The Tools menu will appear.

2. **Click** on **Options**. The Options dialog box will open.

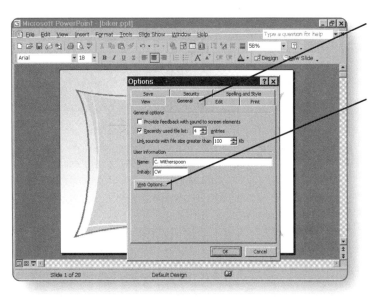

3. **Click** on the **General tab**. The General tab will move to the front.

4. **Click** on **Web Options**. The Web Options dialog box will open.

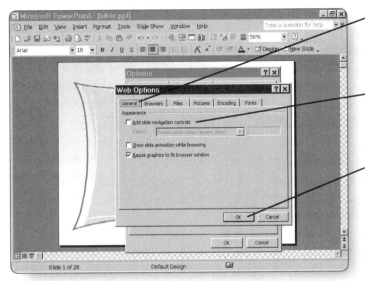

5. Click on the **General tab**. The General tab will move to the front.

6. Click in the **Add slide navigation controls check box**. The check box will be cleared.

7. Click on **OK**. The Options dialog box will reappear.

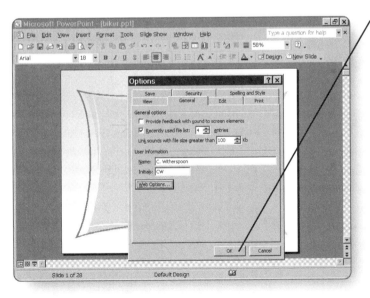

8. Click on **OK**. The notes and outline will not appear in the Web presentation.

Changing Background and Text Colors

If you do want to use the notes and outline in your Web presentation, you have the option of changing the colors of the text and background.

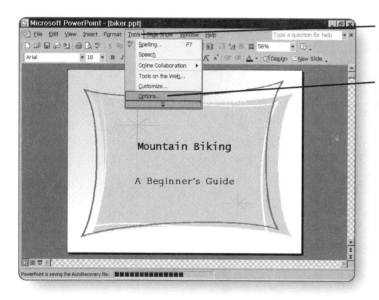

1. Click on **Tools**. The Tools menu will appear.

2. Click on **Options**. The Options dialog box will open.

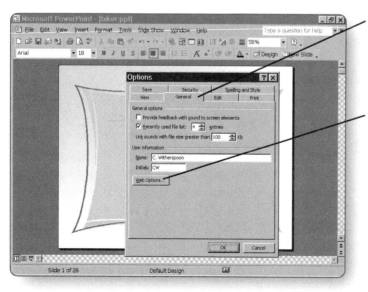

3. Click on the **General tab** if it is not already displayed. The General tab will move to the front.

4. Click on **Web Options**. The Web Options dialog box will open.

5. Click on the **General tab** if it is not already displayed. The General tab will move to the front.

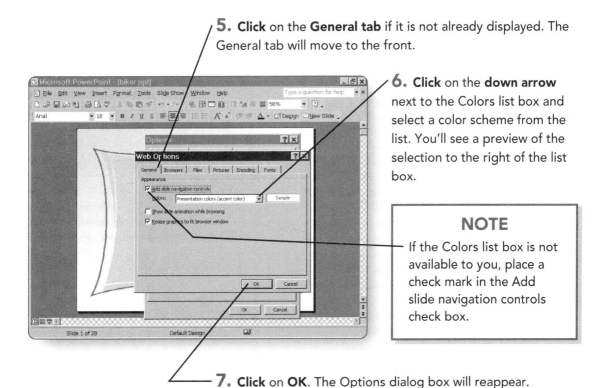

6. Click on the **down arrow** next to the Colors list box and select a color scheme from the list. You'll see a preview of the selection to the right of the list box.

NOTE

If the Colors list box is not available to you, place a check mark in the Add slide navigation controls check box.

7. Click on **OK**. The Options dialog box will reappear.

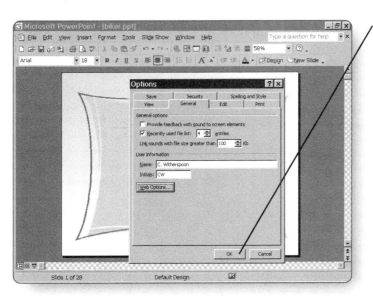

8. Click on **OK**. The colors selected for the text and background will be used when displayed in a Web browser.

Previewing the Presentation Before You Publish

Before you publish your presentation on the World Wide Web where everyone can see it, you'll want to see what it looks like when viewed from a Web browser.

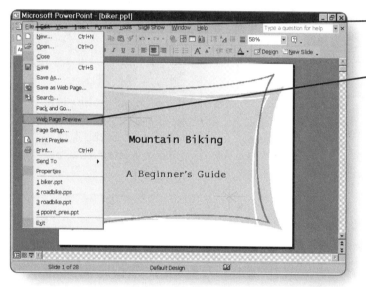

1. Click on **File**. The File menu will appear.

2. Click on **Web Page Preview**. The presentation will open in your default Web browser. If you're using Internet Explorer 5, an additional set of navigation controls will appear along the bottom of the window.

3. Navigate through the **presentation**. Check for navigation ease, spelling errors, and areas that could be improved.

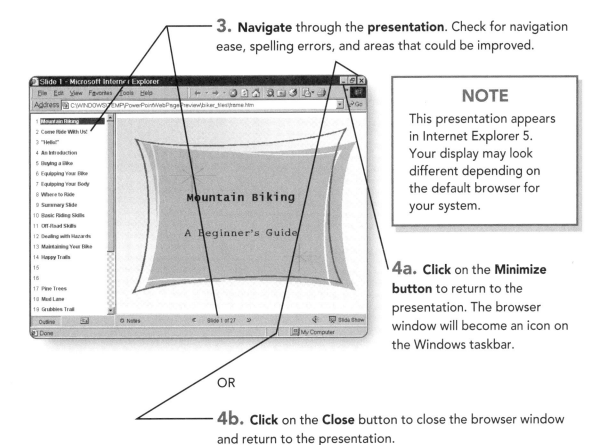

NOTE

This presentation appears in Internet Explorer 5. Your display may look different depending on the default browser for your system.

4a. Click on the **Minimize button** to return to the presentation. The browser window will become an icon on the Windows taskbar.

OR

4b. Click on the **Close** button to close the browser window and return to the presentation.

Publishing the Presentation

When you're satisfied with how your presentation will work on the Web, it's time to publish it. Before you can publish your Web presentation, you'll need an account with an Internet Service Provider (ISP). Your ISP will give you the instructions you need to copy files to your Web space on their server.

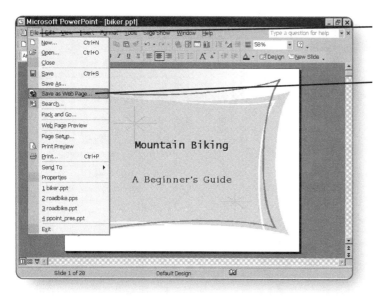

1. **Click** on **File**. The File menu will appear.

2. **Click** on **Save as Web Page**. The Save As dialog box will open.

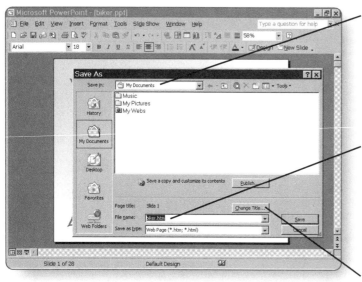

3. **Click** on the **down arrow** next to the Save in list box, and click on the folder to which you want to store the Web presentation. The folder will appear in the list box.

4. **Click** in the **File name text box** and **type** a **different name** for the Web presentation, if you want to distinguish your Web presentation from the original presentation.

5. **Click** on the **Change Title button**. The Set Page Title dialog box will open.

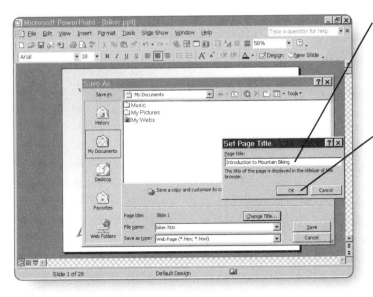

6. **Click** in the **Page title text box** and **type** a **title** for the presentation. This title will appear in the title bar of the Web browser.

7. **Click** on **OK**. The Save As dialog box will reappear.

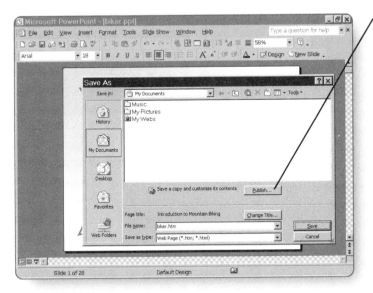

8. **Click** on **Publish**. The Publish as Web Page dialog box will open.

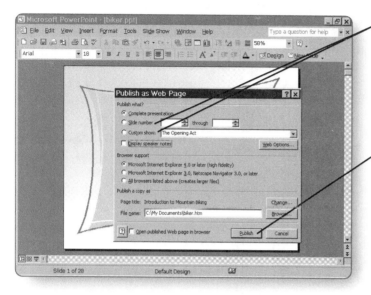

9. To only publish part of the presentation, **click** on either the **Slide number or Custom show option buttons** and **select** the **slides** you want to publish. The slides will be selected.

10. **Click** on **Publish.** Your presentation will be published to the location you specified.

NOTE

Once the Web presentation is stored on your computer, you can publish the presentation to your ISP's Web server using the directions supplied by your ISP. You will need to publish the file and the folder created by PowerPoint. If the file has the name biker.htm, the associated folder is named biker_files.

Part V Review Questions

1. How many items can be stored on the Office Clipboard? See "Using the Office Clipboard" in Chapter 14.

2. What is the easiest way to copy text from an Office application into PowerPoint? See "Dragging and Dropping between Applications" in Chapter 14.

3. When you send a presentation to other people for review, how do those people add comments without changing the formatting or positioning of objects on a slide? See "Commenting on a Presentation" in Chapter 15.

4. What is the purpose of the Notes pane in PowerPoint? See "Using Notes" in Chapter 16.

5. What are the two methods you can use to apply timings to your presentation? See "Rehearsing for the Slide Show" in Chapter 16.

6. How do you make sure a presentation looks as good in grayscale as it does in color? See "Printing in Black and White" in Chapter 17.

7. How do you customize the way handouts appear when printed? See "Creating Handouts" in Chapter 17.

8. If you want to run a slide show on a computer other than the one on which it was created, how do you transfer the presentation file from one computer to another? See "Using the Pack and Go Wizard" in Chapter 18.

9. Is it possible to hide the Notes and Outline panes when viewing the presentation as a Web page? See "Using the Notes and Outline Panes in a Web Presentation" in Chapter 19.

10. How can you be sure your presentation will display on the Web in just the way you want? See "Previewing the Presentation Before You Publish" in Chapter 19.

PART VI

Appendix

A

Using Shortcut Keys

Shortcut keys are a quick and efficient way to execute commands. Shortcut keys increase productivity and decrease the strain caused by excessive mouse usage. Shortcut keys are common to all Microsoft Windows and Office applications, and many shortcut keys are common between applications. This appendix introduces many commonly used shortcut keys. Keep these guides close at hand and practice using the shortcut keys. You'll find that with a little time and patience, you'll be using the keyboard as naturally as you once used the mouse. In this appendix, you'll learn how to:

- Display shortcut keys in the ScreenTips
- Work with presentations
- Navigate the Help system
- Edit text
- Organize an outline
- Move around in a table or presentation

Showing Shortcut Keys in ScreenTips

The menu system lists the shortcut key for a command on the right side of the menu. Shortcut keys can also be displayed in the ScreenTips. By enabling this option, you'll see the shortcut key for a command when you hold the mouse pointer over a toolbar button.

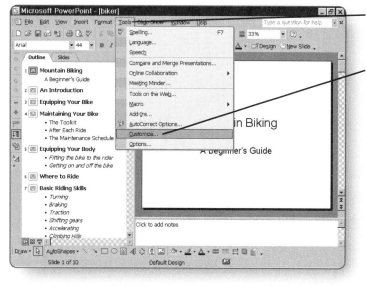

1. **Click** on **Tools**. The Tools menu will appear.

2. **Click** on **Customize**. The Customize dialog box will open.

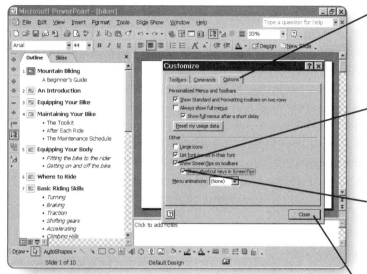

3. **Click** on the **Options tab** if it is not selected when the dialog box opens. The Options tab will come to the top of the stack.

4. **Click** in the **Show ScreenTips on toolbars check box** if it is not selected. A check mark will appear in the check box.

5. **Click** in the **Show shortcut keys in ScreenTips check box**. A check mark will appear in the check box.

6. **Click** on **Close**. The dialog box will close.

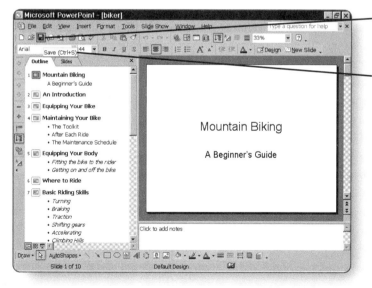

7. **Hold** the **mouse pointer** over a toolbar button.

If a shortcut key is assigned to the command it will appear in the ScreenTip.

Basic Shortcuts

Shortcut keys are easy to remember if you just start with a few shortcuts in the beginning. When you start using these few shortcuts without reverting to the mouse, add a few new shortcut keys. An easy way to start is to get in the habit of holding down the Ctrl key while pressing the S key (Ctrl+S) on a regular basis. This simple shortcut saves the document on which you are working. It's a good idea to save your work every few minutes. The following table lists some other shortcut keys that will help you get your job done faster.

To execute this command	Use this shortcut key
Start a new, blank presentation	Press and hold the Ctrl key and then press the N key (Ctrl+N)
Save a presentation	Ctrl+S
Close a presentation	Ctrl+W
Open a presentation	Ctrl+O
Spell check a presentation	F7
Print a presentation	Ctrl+P
Run a slideshow	F5

Getting Help

If you find yourself using the Help system often, you may want to learn how to start a Help session and navigate through the Help screens without the aid of a mouse. The following tables will help you find the information you need quickly.

Working with the Office Assistant

The Office Assistant is quite comfortable taking commands from shortcut keys. Use the following shortcut keys to call upon the Office Assistant and select from the Assistant's list of possible answers.

To execute this command	Use this shortcut key
Use the What's This? button	Shift+F1
Ask the Office Assistant for help	F1
Open a help topic from the Assistant's list	Alt+*number* (where Alt+1 opens the first topic, Alt+2 opens the second topic, and so on)
See more of the Assistant's list	Alt+Down Arrow
See previous page of the Assistant's list	Alt+Up Arrow
Close the list of Help topics	Esc

Moving Around the Help System

The Help system provides another opportunity for you to learn how to keep your hands off the mouse. The following table lists shortcut keys you can use when navigating the Help files.

To execute this command	Use this shortcut key
Display the Contents tab	Alt+C
Move between the navigation and topic panes	F6
Go to the previous book or topic	Up Arrow
Go to the next book or topic	Down Arrow
Open or close a book or topic	Enter
Display the Answer Wizard tab	Alt+A
Display the Index tab	Alt+I

Outlining Presentations

In Chapter 4, "Organizing the Presentation Outline," you learned how to edit a presentation outline using the Outlining toolbar. The following table lists the shortcut keys you can use to make this job easier.

To execute this command	Use this shortcut key
Insert a new slide	Ctrl+M
Demote an outline item	Alt+Shift+Right Arrow
Promote an outline item	Alt+Shift+Left Arrow
Move a slide down in the outline	Alt+Shift+Down Arrow
Move a slide up in the outline	Alt+Shift+Up Arrow
Show only the title for a selected slide	Alt+Shift+minus sign
Show all of the text for a selected slide	Alt+Shift+plus sign
Collapse an outline to show only the slide titles	Alt+Shift+1
Expand an outline to show all the text on all slides	Alt+Shift+9

Editing Text

As you are adding text to a presentation outline or to the slides, you'll want to try your hand at a few shortcut keys that will make it quicker to select and edit text.

To execute this command	Use this shortcut key
Select one character to the right	Shift+Right Arrow
Select one character to the left	Shift+Left Arrow
Select from cursor to end of word	Ctrl+Shift+Right Arrow
Select from cursor to beginning of word	Ctrl+Shift+Left Arrow
Select from cursor to next line	Shift+Down Arrow
Select from cursor to previous line	Shift+Up Arrow
Delete selected text	Ctrl+X
Copy selected text	Ctrl+C
Paste text from the clipboard	Ctrl+V
Delete one character to the left	Backspace
Delete one word to the left	Ctrl+Backspace
Delete one character to the right	Delete
Delete one word to the right	Ctrl+Delete
Find text on a slide	Ctrl+F
Replace text on a slide	Ctrl+H
Undo editing changes	Ctrl+Z
Redo editing changes	Ctrl+Y

Formatting Text

Formatting text using shortcut keys is easy, and most of these shortcut keys are easy to remember. To format the text, first select the text you want to format and then use the appropriate shortcut keys. The following table lists the most common formatting shortcut keys.

To execute this command	Use this shortcut key
Change the font of the selected text	Ctrl+Shift+F
Make the font larger	Ctrl+Shift+>
Make the font smaller	Ctrl+Shift+<
Make the text bold	Ctrl+B
Underline the text	Ctrl+U
Italicize the text	Ctrl+I
Center a paragraph	Ctrl+E
Left align a paragraph	Ctrl+L
Right align a paragraph	Ctrl+R

Moving Around in a Table or Slide Show

It's a snap to move from cell to cell in a table or from slide to slide in a slide show with a mouse; just one click and you're there! Moving around with the keyboard isn't as intuitive. Use the following table to get around inside tables and slide shows.

To execute this command	Use this shortcut key
Go to the next cell in a table	Tab
Go to the previous cell in a table	Shift+Tab
Move to the next row in a table	Down Arrow
Move to the previous row in a table	Up Arrow
Move to the next slide in a slide show	Spacebar
Go to the previous slide in a slide show	Backspace
Display a specific slide in a slide show	Type the slide number and press Enter
End the slide show	Esc

Glossary

3-D. Having or appearing to have three dimensions: width, height, and depth.

Accessibility. The ease of use and access to the program is enhanced to aid those with limited vision or impaired movement.

Agenda slide. A slide that lists items for the agenda or headings for main sections of your presentation.

Animation. The addition of special effects such as movement or sound to objects in your presentation.

Annotate. To draw or write on a slide during a presentation using the annotation pen.

Answer Wizard. The Answer Wizard lets you formulate your question in your own words, and then automatically directs you to the proper place within Help for your answer.

AutoShape. A ready-made shape for you to use in your presentations. The AutoShapes menu can be found on the Drawing toolbar.

Bitmap. A graphic file with its graphic information stored pixel by pixel. Bitmap images cannot be directly converted into PowerPoint images.

Bullet. A character, number, or graphic object used to delineate special sections of the text.

Callouts. These are text additions to the slide that point to specific items and give information about them. In PowerPoint, these are drawing objects that may be sized, rotated, and otherwise manipulated along with the information contained within them.

Caption. An alternative description of a picture, chart, or other graphic that may be used in a presentation to indicate the content of the picture, chart, and so on.

Chart. A graphic representation of a data array, such as a pie-shaped graphic sliced to show spending or budget contributions.

Clip art. The name applied to various graphics that are freely available for you to use in presentations.

Clip Organizer. This contains a large number of graphic objects and pictures that you can use to enhance and illustrate your slides.

Collapse. When working in Outline view, clicking on the (-) at the beginning of a major heading will hide the subheadings shown indented below the main heading. This can be used to show an Outline view that has only major headings.

Color scheme. A set of eight colors that you can use in combination within your presentation to give a uniform appearance.

Comments. Notes added to the slides by you, or perhaps others, that are not automatically shown with the slides in the presentation. They are separate from the slides and may be turned on or off.

Connector lines. Three types of lines that you may use to connect objects: straight, angled, and curved. These remain attached to the object when it is moved and may be reshaped by handles on the connector lines to make rearranging objects easier.

Crop. Trimming the horizontal and vertical edges of a picture using the cropping tool on the Picture toolbar.

Drag and drop. Moving or otherwise manipulating an object by clicking on the left mouse button and "dragging" the mouse pointer until the object is placed where desired.

Drawing object. A text box, WordArt drawing, AutoShape, or other clip art object that you can insert into a picture.

Duplicate. You can make more than one copy of a slide for the same presentation or for use in other presentations by selecting the object to duplicate and then clicking on Duplicate on the Edit menu.

Embedded objects. Information inserted into a file from another file (source file) that becomes part of the file into which it is inserted (destination file) after it becomes embedded. Double-clicking on the embedded object launches the original application in which the object was created.

Emboss. A shadow effect available on the Drawing toolbar that you may apply to drawing objects to give them 3-D effects.

Engrave. Effect on the Drawing toolbar that gives texture effects to drawing objects.

Expand. When working in the Outline view, clicking on the (+) sign beside a major heading in an outline will display the subheadings cascading down in outline format.

Fill. You can fill drawing objects with solid or shaded colors, textures, or even pictures.

Flip. You can rotate an object 90 degrees in either direction, and you can flip it horizontally or vertically.

Font. A family of type characters all of the same design, such as Garamond or Times New Roman.

Footer. The text at the bottom of the page that reflects the page number, the document name, or other similar information and that prints on the bottom of every page.

Format. The organized way in which objects and text are placed on a page or slide.

Freeform object. An object created by selecting a freeform shape from the AutoShapes menu and then dragging and reshaping it with the handles.

Gradient. A way of adding a pattern to an object to make it appear shaded.

Graph. A visual representation of an array of data organized to show trends.

Grayscale. A method that converts color images into black and white. Different amounts of black and white are combined to produce shades of gray that more closely represent the different shades of color in the image.

Grid. A space with evenly spaced lines (often invisible) in which objects may be dragged and then inserted exactly by having their boundaries snap to a grid line.

Gridline. A line upon a grid on which drawing objects may be exactly placed by using the snap function.

Group. To assemble drawing objects together and bind them so that they can all be manipulated together and still maintain their relative positions regarding each other.

Guide. Guides are available to help you align objects and text on your slide.

Handle. A diamond-shaped handle is used to change the shape of most AutoShapes;

there are also handles on the connecting lines to allow you to move drawing objects.

Header. A text box or graphic that is inserted on the top of each page in a document with information such as the company name, date, document title, or page number.

Hue. You can change the color of the shadow fills by clicking on the Shadow Style button on the Drawing toolbar and then clicking on Shadow Settings. On the Shadow Settings toolbar, click on the arrow next to Shadow Color.

Hyperlink. A link from a place in your document to another document (either in a separate file or on the Web) or another place inside your document.

Import. To bring text or graphics into PowerPoint from other programs for inclusion as a PowerPoint object in a presentation or stored in the PowerPoint clip art gallery.

Kiosk. A standalone computer that plays a presentation on a continuous basis. A kiosk is usually unattended or used as a part of a display, and the presentation is set up to automatically move from slide to slide.

Line art. Graphics that are redrawn on the screen from a set of vectors contained in a file as opposed to a pixel-by-pixel graphic map such as a bitmap.

Linked objects. Objects (information) in a file that remain connected to, and receive updates from, the original application in which they were created.

Macro. A small script used to simplify repetitive tasks and reduce keyboard strokes.

Multimedia. Elements such as animation, music, and video that you can add to your presentation.

Normal view. In Normal view, three panes are visible: the Outline pane, Slide pane, and Notes pane. The ability to focus on all aspects of the presentation simultaneously is helpful. Dragging the pane borders can change the size of the different panes.

Notes Master. There are masters for both the Notes and Handouts. The master can contain the header and footer information or any picture or icon that you want to appear on all the Notes pages or handouts.

Office Assistant. A handy little artificial-intelligence-enhanced assistant that can help you sort through the Help files for the specific information you request and that spontaneously offers help with tasks.

Organization chart. PowerPoint has a program that builds organization charts, offering tools and templates for you to create, edit, and modify the charts.

Outline view. A view of a document showing section headings and detailed subheadings in outline form. Text may be moved and the overall order of elements changed by dragging and dropping the outline heads in another spot in the document.

Overhead. A slide shown with an overhead projector on a screen.

Placeholder. A small, dotted-line box that marks the position of text or objects on a slide. You can add text by typing it into the placeholder.

Presentation. An organized collection of text and graphics displayed to an audience to orient, teach, advertise, market, and so on.

Presentation broadcasting. You can broadcast presentations over the Web and make them accessible to viewers in remote locations.

Preview. You may preview all your Web pages and video and animation effects before using them in a presentation.

Regroup. You may use the Drawing toolbar to reassemble objects that previously were grouped. Select Draw and then Regroup.

Rotate. To turn an object on its axis, such as rotating a picture or a graphic on a slide.

Scan. Pictures can be imported into PowerPoint from a scanner or a digital camera if the hardware is TWAIN-compatible.

Shadow. You can apply shadows to drawing objects by selecting the Shadow Style button on the Drawing toolbar.

Slide Master. PowerPoint comes with a Slide Master slide. The Slide Master controls text characteristics, background color, and special effects, such as shadowing and bullet style. It also contains placeholders for text and layout attributes such as headers and footers.

Slide show. An ordered presentation of slides, often accompanied by narration or animation and other special effects.

Slide Sorter view. In Slide Sorter view, the whole presentation is shown in miniature. You can add slide transitions, rearrange slides, and preview them in this view.

Spell check. You may spell check your documents in PowerPoint as you do in other Office applications. You can have PowerPoint check spelling as you type or have the spell check done all at one time.

Style checker. PowerPoint automatically checks your presentation for consistency and style. The Office Assistant must be turned on to have this feature available.

Summary Slide. By clicking the Summary Slide button on the Slide Sorter toolbar, you can create a slide that contains all the agenda items for the presentation.

Table. Tables are handy ways of including data and other objects in your presentation. You can format a table of your own or you can import tables from other programs, such as Microsoft Word.

Text Box tool. You can enter text easily with the Text Box tool on the Drawing toolbar.

Transparent. You can set transparent areas in objects such as pictures. You can make the background of the picture transparent and just show certain objects in the picture, without the background.

Undo. A handy function accessible by the button on the Standard toolbar shaped like a left-curving arrow. Should you need to do so, you may undo any mouse or keyboard action and its result by clicking on the Undo button.

Ungroup. You can remove objects grouped in a drawing object by clicking on the Ungroup selection found in the Draw menu selection on the Drawing toolbar.

Voice narration. You may add voice narration to your presentation in PowerPoint. If you do so, the narration can be archived and shown later or used as a Web presentation.

Zoom. To move the viewer's perspective closer or farther away either by enlarging a detail (Zoom in) or by displaying the complete object (Zoom out).

Index

A

action buttons, applying, 292–295
Action Settings dialog box, 300
ActiveX, installing, 44
adding. *See also* inserting
    clip art, 116–118
    Clipboard items, 219–221
    columns, 146
    comments, 236
    diagram shapes, 175–177
    footers, 106–107
    items to outlines, 60–61
    line art, 127–130
    members to organization charts, 163–164
    notes to slides, 244–245
    reviewers' changes, 238–241
    rows, 146
    slide text, 77–79
    slides, 88
    text to diagrams, 172–175
    text to tables, 143–145
    voice-over narration, 260–262
aligning. *See also* moving
    graphics, 121–122
    Office Shortcut Bar, 9
    slide text, 80–81
    slides, 85–91

animation
    customizing, 196–197
    slide shows, 186–196
    slide transitions, 193–195
    starting, 192
    text, 187–193
applications. *See also* Office
    e-mail, 298–299
    moving items between, 223–225
applying
    action buttons, 292–295
    animation, 186–187
    backgrounds, 108–109
    hidden slides, 253
    notes, 244–245
    Notes Master, 247–249
    Notes/Outline panes, 301–305
    reviewers' changes, 238–241
    styles to diagrams, 178–181
    templates, 41–48
    3-D styles, 130
Ask a Question, 24–26
audiences, browsing presentations, 285–286
audio. *See* sound
AutoContent Wizard, 36–40
AutoFormat, 178–179
AutoPreview, 187

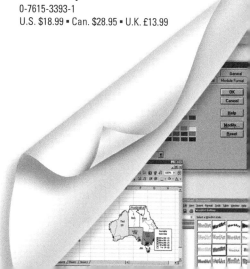